UNDERSTAND YOUR ACCOUNTS

981/2148
54 PRIEST MAN POINT
RAINHILL WAY
BOW E.3

Understand Your Accounts

A St J Price FCA

Kogan Page

First published in 1978 by Lynxplan (Sheffield) Ltd
This revised edition first published in 1979 by
Kogan Page Ltd
120 Pentonville Road, London N1

Printed in Great Britain by
Anchor Press Limited, Tiptree, Essex.

Hardback ISBN 0 85038 205 X
Paperback ISBN 0 85038 199 1

Contents

Introduction

Understand Your Accounts is the first part, reprinted verbatim, of the second edition of a larger book *Profit from Figures, Financial Control for Non Accountants*. The latter is virtually the only easy-to-read book which covers the subject thoroughly, yet simply, and which gives practical examples and exercises including a full set of budget schedules. From comments received in my own experience of using it as lecture material, I know that readers find it a valuable book.

However, some people are a little daunted by the scope of *Profit from Figures*. Accounts are so much of a mystery that they prefer to take one step at a time, to grasp the meaning of their annual accounts before tackling budgets. *Understand Your Accounts* shows you how to read a balance sheet. It strips the mystery away from figures and helps you to ask more sensible questions about them, which gives you better value from your accountant.

Do you find figures difficult?

Every time I run one of my seminars based on *Profit from Figures* I am reminded of how, to many people, numbers are 'difficult'. Often they tell me that their minds go blank when faced with figures. If this applies to you too, relax. Interpreting and using figures is mostly common sense, and people find it a problem largely because it is badly taught.

Understand Your Accounts includes some new material and many minor revisions, as prepared for the new edition of my larger book. Already proven in practice, I am sure that it will give you the confidence to cope with numbers.

How to use this book

If you find difficulty with any point, leave it and carry on. Read the whole book through quickly and then revise it more slowly. This is the easiest way to master any problems. Each section contains questions or exercises to check your understanding.

A St J Price, FCA
York
February 1979

Section 1:
Why Do You Need Financial Control?

Why does financial control matter?

Business is about money. Without money, no business can operate. Whatever other reasons you may have for being in business, to make money is vital — without money your business will fail.

To make money, you must successfully organise the financial aspects of your business. You must ensure that:

(a) you earn enough profit to stay in business
(b) your profit results in enough cash in the bank to pay the bills.

As we shall see later, profit does not necessarily mean cash. Profit can be tied up in stocks, debtors, equipment, etc and, if this results in a shortage of cash to pay the bills, you may have to close down or sell out.

Thus profits will only keep the business going if they produce enough cash, and they will only do so if you have good financial control. In contrast, a concern which has reserves of cash built up in past years can survive as long as good financial control enables it to eke out its cash. So it is just as important to plan for cash as it is for profit.

What is financial control?

Financial control means:

knowing where you are   — annual accounts
planning where you are going — budgets
making sure you get there   — regular progress reports

A sound understanding of where you are now is the basis for all financial control.

Your accounts are a goldmine of information

There is valuable information to be found in your figures, but they cannot talk for themselves. You must read them to obtain it; you may even have to dig deeply. To extract this information you must understand the basis of the accounts. The objective of this book is to show you how to cope with figures, and extract the gold from them. I do **not** try to turn you into an accountant.

Why does my accountant not do all this for me?

Well, it is your money, is it not? (Even if you merely run a part of someone else's business, your personal success depends partly on the financial result.) The interest must come from you in the first place. Accountants, whether outside auditors or internal colleagues, are busy people. They are human too, believe it or not! With many demands made on them, they naturally do most for the person who takes an informed interest in his figures — he is much easier to help than the one who has to be prodded into looking at the numbers.

Questions on Section 1 *(Check your answers with the text)*
☐ What are the objectives of financial control?
☐ What does financial control consist of?

Section 2:
What Do Annual Accounts Consist of?

Annual accounts consist of a *profit and loss account* and a *balance sheet.* The profit and loss account shows what has happened during the year and whether the result is a profit or a loss; the balance sheet shows where the business has then got to, ie what it owns and what it owes — its assets and its liabilities.

These accounts state in formal terms what you no doubt do informally in managing your personal affairs. During the month you earn so much in salary, or draw so much from your business, and spend this on food, rent or mortgage, clothes, the cinema, beer, etc. At the end of the month you add up what you have left. You may have some money left over; perhaps you have no cash left or you owe some to other people or to your bank. The point is that you need to know whether you have spent more or less money than you have earned in that month. This is your personal profit and loss account — a statement of what has happened during the month.

In summing up your affairs, you will take into account any exceptional spending on furniture or hi-fi equipment, for example, things that will be of use to you for some time ahead. You could even draw up a personal balance sheet. Most of your spending would have no further value to you, but things such as furniture, clothes and so on could be listed and a figure put on them. You could thus show whether your net worth in terms of things owned and money in the bank was greater or less at the end of the month than at the beginning.

The profit and loss account

The terms 'trading account' and 'appropriation account' are jargon for sections of the profit and loss account.

The profit and loss account shows the profit or loss made during the period covered (a month, quarter, year, etc). This is after allowing for bills owed but not yet paid (creditors), amounts owed to the business but not yet received (debtors) and sums, such as rent, paid for periods not yet finished (payments in advance).

The balance sheet

The balance sheet shows the value of the business at the date to which the profit and loss account was made up. It lists the assets — buildings, equipment, stocks, debtors, cash, etc, and the liabilities — loans, creditors, bank overdraft, etc. The difference between the two totals is the owner's interest in the business. If it is a limited company this is called share capital and reserves: if it is a partnership or a sole trader it is shown as partners/owners capital and current accounts.

The owner's interest is in fact the original cash put into the business, plus profits earned since after tax, less cash drawn out.

The next two sections explain the profit and loss account and the balance sheet in detail, define the accounting jargon and show you which are the key figures and ratios. You do not have to learn all the accountancy language but you do need enough understanding of the more important terms to be able to read your accounts and discuss them with your accountant.

Who sees the accounts (apart from the owners or shareholders)?

Every business needs accounts in order to agree its tax liability. In addition, a limited company must file a copy of its accounts with the Registrar of Companies, where it is available for public inspection.

The bank manager may ask to see a copy, particularly if he has lent money to the business. The VAT inspector also has the right to ask to see the accounts.

How often are accounts needed?

Normally accounts are prepared annually but this may vary. Progressive businessmen use their accounts to help them run their business. It is often helpful to have half-yearly, quarterly or even monthly accounts in order to provide up-to-date information on the business.

How frequently you need accounts will depend on your business. In many cases, the small businessman does not need complete figures during the year. Provided that he has an overall grasp of his annual results, and he has projected a budget for the coming year, he can keep track of what is happening by comparing the key figures against his forecast. There are usually only two or three such figures, which alter from month to month, such as sales, purchase of goods for resale, and wages. Often he can keep track of these during the year without formal accounts.

Questions on Section 2 *(Check your answers with the text)*
☐ What is the difference between a profit and loss account and a balance sheet?
☐ Does the profit and loss account show:
  (a) the value of expenses incurred (ie commitments made), or
  (b) those actually spent (cash paid out)?

AN EXAMPLE OF A PROFIT AND LOSS ACCOUNT OF A SMALL BUSINESS – THE XYZ COMPANY

Profit and loss account for the year ended 30th June

	Last year £		This year £		
Sales		39000			47500
Opening stock (1st July last year)	4300		4800		
Add purchases	29960		38260		
	34260		43060		
Less closing stock (30th June this year)	4800		6500		
Cost of goods sold		29460			36560
Gross profit 23% (24.5% last year)		9540			10940
Expenses					
Staff wages	1400		1700		
Rent	1040		1040		
Rates	380		460		
Electricity	250		300		
Telephone	70		80		
Insurance	70		80		
Professional fees	80		100		
Motor expenses	160		200		
Advertising	240		400		
Repairs	100		150		
Stationery and postage	200		250		
Sundry expenses	110		140		
Total expenses		4100			4900
Interest: loan	100		100		
bank overdraft	300		400		
				500	
Depreciation: equipment, fixtures and fittings	440		440		
motor vehicle	400		400		
				840	
Net profit before tax		£4200			£4700
The net profit can be re-stated as					
Proprietor's salary		2400			3000
'Super profit'		1800			1700
		£4200			£4700

Section 3:
The Profit and Loss Account

Introduction

As explained in Section 2, the profit and loss account shows how much profit (or loss) you have made. It starts with sales, deducts the cost of sales to show the gross profit, then deducts expenses to show the net profit (or loss). Each of these headings is explained below. The notes should be read in conjunction with the example opposite of a profit and loss account for a typical small business.

'Last year' and 'this year'

The figures for last year are given to show how the results for this year (the year just ended) have changed. The comparisons are very useful in helping you to understand the progress of your business.

Sales (or takings or turnover) £47,500

This is the value of goods sold (or services performed in, say, a hairdressing salon or a contracting business). It does not include VAT because the latter belongs to the Government. It is net of any credits to customers for returns, discounts, etc, though these could be shown separately if significant.

If you sell on credit you count as sales the value of goods despatched or services performed during the period, *not* just the cash you have received.

Cost of goods sold £36,560

From your sales, you must deduct the cost of providing or producing what you sell. This is called cost of goods sold and is the next figure down in the right-hand column.

Most accountants use the term 'cost of sales' rather than 'cost of goods sold'. Both terms mean the same but I have found that laymen understand the latter term more easily.

If you sell goods, your cost of goods sold is the cost to you of the items you sell. If you provide services, your cost of sales is any material you use. If you employ staff whose time you sell, such as in a repair workshop, your cost of goods sold may be mostly wages.

Cost of goods sold therefore means those of your costs which vary directly in proportion to your sales. In most businesses the only cost which varies directly with sales is goods purchased or produced. You arrive at the value sold or used up in sales during the year by adding to the stocks you began with the goods you purchased, and then deducting the stocks you have left. This calculation is inset in the left-hand column between 'sales' and 'cost of goods sold'. The figures are explained below.

Stocks — opening £48,000; closing £6500

The stock figure is the value of the goods held for sale to customers or of materials held for use in performing your services.

Stocks are valued at cost net of VAT, *not* at selling price. If you valued them at selling price you would be taking profit on them before you had sold them. Any items which are old, obsolete, in poor condition or held in excessive quantities in relation to sales should be priced down to realistic values.

Purchases £38,260

This is the value of goods net of VAT received between the

two stock-taking dates, *not* the total of cash paid to creditors. It is net of any returns to suppliers. Discounts received from suppliers may be shown separately if important.

Gross profit £10,940

This is a key figure. It is the profit per item sold or service rendered after charging your cost of sales but before paying all your fixed costs such as rent, rates, electricity, etc. Since your cost of goods sold should be roughly constant as a percentage of sales, so should your gross profit.

Gross profit is very important. If you do not have the right profit at the gross level, you cannot have it at the net. Suppose gross profit is 25 per cent of sales and net profit 10 per cent, a 1 per cent variation from 25 per cent to 24 per cent looks trivial — it's only 4 per cent of your gross profit: but the same 1 per cent becomes 10 per cent of your net profit (1 per cent on 10 per cent).

In practice gross profit is never a constant percentage of sales, for various reasons. For example, as your sales rise you should obtain better buying terms; on the other hand, stock losses can make a large hole in your profit.

Some causes of stock losses are:

- damaged goods destroyed or sold off at lower prices
- natural losses by evaporation, etc
- inaccurate measuring of quantities sold or pricing errors
- human errors by you in invoicing where goods sold on credit or by supplier when bought on credit
- fraud by customers (shoplifting, etc)
- fraud by suppliers (wrong deliveries or inaccurate invoicing)
- fraud by staff (cash or goods taken; goods supplied to friends at wrong prices, etc).

Expenses (wages and other overheads as listed in the example)

These are the expenses of operating the business for the period. In some cases, such as wages, the cost is usually the same as cash paid out. But for bills, such as telephone bills, which are incurred on credit, the cost for the period is the bills which relate to that period, *not* just those which happen to have been paid during it.

Similarly, some expenses are paid in advance. Rent, rates and insurance are examples, and for these, the cost is the proportion relating to the period of the accounts, not the total paid out.

Depreciation £840

Depreciation is a different sort of cost to the other expenses: there is no invoice in the books for it but it is a cost nonetheless. Many assets used in the business wear out over a period. Plant, equipment, fixtures, fittings and vehicles are examples. The objective of depreciation is to charge against profits the cost of the asset over its working life. When it is either sold or scrapped, the depreciation charged up to that date therefore represents profit set aside to replace it.

Note that the profit set aside may not be represented by actual cash. The cash may already have been used to finance other fixed assets, stocks, debtors, etc. The reasons why profit is not necessarily the same as cash will become clearer as you read subsequent sections.

Note also that since estimates or averages have to be used for each kind of asset, the amount is only an intelligent guess, not a precise forecast.

The depreciation is based upon historic cost. The price of a replacement item may have risen substantially due to inflation, technological advances, etc. So you might need to make extra provision for the replacement of assets over and above normal depreciation.

Net profit before tax £4700

I re-state this as you can see in the example. Proprietor's (or director's) salary represents the wage of the owner manager. It is important to charge a realistic figure comparable to that which you could obtain in ordinary employment. The balance is then your 'super profit' which is the real return you obtain from your investment in the business. It is the correct figure to compare with the return you could obtain by selling the business, investing the proceeds and taking a job. Express your 'super profit' as a percentage of your interest in the business and you have the real reward for all the extra sweat of being the boss.

Questions on Section 3 *(Check your answers with the text)*

☐ Does the sales figure include VAT?

☐ Does the stock valuation include VAT?

☐ Is the purchases figure:

(a) value of goods received in the period
   or
(b) value of invoices received in the period
   or
(c) total of cash paid to suppliers in the period?

☐ What does the cost of goods sold figure represent?

☐ What are the causes of stock losses (give at least five)

☐ What is gross profit?

AN EXAMPLE OF A BALANCE SHEET OF A SMALL BUSINESS – THE XYZ COMPANY

Balance sheet at 30th June

Last year		Net book value Start of year	Bought in year	Sales in year	Depreciation for year	This year Net book value End of year
£	*Fixed assets*	£	£	£	£	£
2040	Equipment	2040	1200	200	340	2700
900	Fixtures and fittings	900	150	150	100	800
1200	Vehicle	1200	–	–	400	800
4140		4140	1350	350	840	4300
3000	*Goodwill*					3000
	Current assets					
6000	Stocks (trade £6500; other £300)				6800	
900	Accounts receivable (debtors)				1000	
260	Payments in advance				300	
7160						8100
14300	*Total assets*					15400
	Less					
	Current liabilities					
1200	Accounts payable (creditors)				1300	
1200	Future tax payable				1500	
2400	Bank overdraft				3000	
4800						5800
1000	*Long-term loan*					1000
£8500	*Proprietor's interest in the business*					£8600
	Represented by:					
8300	Balance of capital at start of year					8500
3200	Add profit for year (after taxation of £1200)					3500
11500						12000
3000	Deduct drawings					3400
£8500	Balance of capital at end of year					£8600

Section 4:
The Balance Sheet

Read this section in conjunction with the example of a balance sheet for the XYZ Company. If you own or work for a limited company, you will also need to read the next section, 'The accounts of a limited company', since there are differences between the accounts for sole traders or partnerships and those for limited companies. You should read this section first, however, because various points are common to all businesses.

As already explained in Section 1, the balance sheet shows where the business has got to at the date on which the profit and loss account ends. It is, if you like, a snapshot of the business at that moment. In contrast, the profit and loss account can be likened to a moving film of the events during the year. There is no rigid rule about the order in which a balance sheet is set out. This example begins with what the business owns, its assets, and deducts its liabilities, to arrive at the net value, the proprietor's interest; sometimes, however, the latter (for a limited company the share capital) is shown at the top.

There are three kinds of assets: fixed, intangible and current.

Fixed assets

These are the items which the business buys to retain for use over a long period, rather than to resell at a profit. They are usually kept until they wear out, become obsolete or are no longer suitable for the business. Examples are buildings, plant, equipment, fixtures and fittings and vehicles.

The layout shown here for fixed assets is that usually adopted for sole traders or partnerships (for limited companies, see the next section). The net book value is the balance remaining after deducting, from the NBV at the start of the year, the depreciation as shown in the profit and loss account. Additions and sales of assets during the year are also shown and the depreciation is calculated on the starting net book value after deducting any sales plus a proportion for items bought during the year. This is called the 'reducing balance' method of depreciating and, since a percentage of the reducing total is written off, the assets are never fully depreciated. It is simple to use, and it is not necessary to keep records of each item in order to show when it is written off.

Intangible assets and goodwill

These include goodwill, patent, trade-mark or royalty rights and other items for which cash is paid but which have no tangible form.

Goodwill

In the example, the proprietor of the business paid £3000 for goodwill when he bought it. That is to say, the price he paid exceeded by £3000 the value of the net assets he took over. Net assets are fixtures and fittings, equipment, stock, debtors, etc, less any liabilities to creditors etc, for which he accepted responsibility.

People are often confused about goodwill. It is not an identifiable asset with its own value. It is in effect a balancing figure arrived at as follows.

Say you are offered a business earning a net profit of £3500. You are prepared to pay 1½ years' profits for it, plus stock at valuation. You are therefore buying the leasehold, fixed assets and goodwill for £5250. If the fixed assets are valued at £3000 you are paying £2250 for the right to the leasehold (not usually separated from goodwill) and the goodwill. If any debtors or creditors were taken over they would, of course, be a part of the calculation.

However, this is a half-truth. The value of the fixed assets always depends upon the view you take of them. If you value them for use as they stand in a going concern, they are worth far more than if you tried to sell them off as surplus. So the balancing figure taken as the value of goodwill is purely arbitrary. One cannot value goodwill for itself — only as a consequence of deciding what one will pay for a given amount of profit and then deducting one's valuation of fixed assets, and current assets if applicable, from the price paid.

Current assets

These are the items arising and constantly changing in the course of trading. Examples are stocks which convert into debtors which become cash. Note that 'other' stocks are such items as stationery or fuel. 'Trade' stocks are goods for resale.

Similarly, liabilities are long-term or short-term.

Long-term liabilities

These are amounts repayable over the year ahead such as loans, mortgages, etc; but *not* a bank overdraft because this is repayable on demand.

Current liabilities

These are amounts repayable more than a year ahead such as loans, mortgages, etc; but *not* a bank overdraft because this is repayable on demand.

Accounts receivable or payable (debtors and creditors)

A debtor owes you money. You owe money to a creditor. It may help you to distinguish between them if you recall that it is the creditors of a business who force it into liquidation. One talks of a creditor's winding up, not a debtor's one.

EXAMPLE OF A HORIZONTAL LAYOUT – THE XYZ COMPANY

Balance sheet at 30th June

Last year	This year		
£	£		
			Capital
8300	8500		Balance on capital account at start of year
3200	3500		Add profit for year (after taxation of £1200)
11500	12000		
3000	3400		Deduct drawings
£8500	£8600		Proprietor's interest in the business
1000	1000		*Long-term loan*
			Current liabilities
1200		1300	Creditors
1200		1500	Future tax payable
2400		3000	Bank overdraft
4800	5800		
£14300	£15400		*Total liabilities*

Last year				This year
				Net book value
£		Cost	Accumulated depreciation	£
	Fixed assets	£	£	
2040	Equipment	3400	700	2700
900	Fixtures and fittings	1000	200	800
1200	Vehicle	1600	800	800
4140		6000	1700	4300
3000	Goodwill			3000
	Current assets			
6000	Stocks (trade £6500: other £300)		6800	
900	Debtors		1000	
260	Payments in advance		300	
7160				8100
£14300	*Total assets*			£15400

Proprietor's interest in the business

This represents the cash originally put in plus profits, less taxation and drawings and any losses. In the balance sheet of a limited company it is shown as share capital and reserves, the total of which belongs to the shareholders. Individual directors, who may or may not be the shareholders, may have amounts owing to them on current account as well but these sums are current liabilities. 'Drawings' of profit for a company are dividends to the shareholders. If the directors own the company, they may of course draw profit as salaries rather than as dividends.

In a partnership, and sometimes for a sole trader, a distinction is made between permanent capital and current account balances of profits not drawn. The total of capital and current balances is then the proprietor's interest.

Expressed slightly differently, the owner's interest is the value of what the business owns less what it owes to outsiders.

'Vertical' or 'horizontal' layout

The proprietor's interest is a liability of the business to him. This is why, in a 'horizontal' layout of a balance sheet, it appears in the liabilities. The same figures used for the sample 'vertical' balance sheet are re-laid out in the 'horizontal' layout as per the second sample because many accountants use this form. The layout is simply a matter of preference.

Questions on Section 4 (*Check your answers with the text*)
What are:
☐ fixed assets
☐ intangible assets and goodwill
☐ current assets
☐ long-term liabilities
☐ current liabilities
☐ proprietor's interest in the business?

Section 5:
The Accounts of a Limited Company

This section concerns those who trade as a limited company or who work for one. Please read section 4 first, however, because points common to both are not repeated.

The accounts of a limited company vary from those of a sole trader or partnership in order to reflect its different legal status. These notes discuss how. The figures quoted assume that, some years on, the XYZ Company has prospered and has been incorporated as a company. For convenience many of the previous figures have been multiplied by 10 to up-date them.

The profit and loss account of a limited company

There are two major differences from the example already shown. Firstly, the directors, being employees of the company, are paid salaries. This expense is shown either with or adjacent to staff costs and amounts to £17,000. Assuming the present profit of the business before the director's pay to be £47,000, this leaves a net profit for the company of £30,000.

Secondly, this profit is then dealt with through the profit and loss appropriation account. This is a continuation of the main profit and loss account and shows what happens to the pre-tax profit already arrived at. Thus:

£		£
24000	Net profit before tax	30000
9000	Less corporation tax	12000
15000	Net profit after tax	18000
1000	Less preference dividend	1000
	Ordinary dividend interim already paid £3000	
6500	final proposed £4000	7000
7500	Balance of profit undistributed for year	10000
21500	Add balance brought forward from previous years	29000
29000	Balance of profit undistributed carried forward (see balance sheet)	39000

This example assumes that there are outside shareholders in the XYZ Company Ltd who require dividends on their shares. If the shareholders are all directors, they will normally prefer to draw the profits as directors' salaries, rather than dividends, for tax reasons. Shares are explained later and dividends in the next section.

In this example, the company has a profit of £18,000 available after tax for distribution to shareholders or for retention in the company. Dividends either paid or proposed take £8000, leaving £10,000 retained to add to the accumulated balance of previous retentions.

Is the profit retention of £10,000 cash in the bank?

This £10,000 retained is not necessarily cash in the bank. It may well have been already used to finance increased stocks or receivables (debtors). The reason for this is explained in later sections.

How much profit should be retained?

Today you cannot take out your profits. You must leave money in your business to finance it, especially if your sales are growing. And you must build up resources for a rainy day.

The requirement to retain the profit varies of course from company to company and, to some extent, from trade to trade. Some industries, particularly manufacturers, have to invest far more heavily in new equipment and require more working capital to stay in business than do others. More sales means more stock, more credit to customers and so on, all of which absorbs cash as working capital. This is further explained in later sections.

Industries such as the furniture, building and construction industries tend to be cyclical, with good and bad years succeeding each other, as the economy changes. Such companies cannot pay out a high proportion of profits as dividends in good years if they are to maintain the dividend in poor ones. They tend therefore to retain a high proportion of profit in the good years to provide a cushion for the bad times when they may have difficulty in earning enough to 'cover' the dividend.

A few industries, such as the retailing industry tend to pay out a higher proportion of profit because they are more static. The business is more stable and swings in profits are less violent. If the company is well run, much of a retailer's working capital is provided by credit from his suppliers. A good proportion of his stocks can be sold for cash before or around the date on which he has to pay for them. He can therefore afford to pay out a higher proportion of profits and indeed often needs to do so because the attraction of his shares to an investor is more likely to be a secure steady income than the prospect of rapidly increasing profits.

Of course, the best companies in any particular industry tend to be exceptions to such general statements. Equally the financial situation of the company often dictates the policy. It may be necessary to plough back more profit than usual for several years to finance expansion. On the other hand, a high dividend may have to be paid in order to persuade the shareholders to invest fresh capital to pay for expansion because there is no way that the company can generate enough cash from its existing business.

The balance sheet of a limited company

This balance sheet is similar in outline to that of a sole

trader or partnership but there are various differences in detail.

What is share capital?

It will help you to understand these notes if we deal first with share capital. It is not the first figure in the example but, since you must know what it is in order to follow the points made about other entries, it is dealt with first. So we start with the shareholders' interest.

Share capital — ordinary shares £1500

The share capital of a company represents money put in by the shareholders to finance it. As a receipt for the money it issues 'shares'. These shares can be sold by one shareholder to another or to a third party. If the company's shares are quoted on the Stock Exchange, this is of course easily done.

Sometimes shares are issued in return for assets transferred to the company rather than for cash paid into its bank account.

If the company is a private one, the transfer of its shares is often subject to control by the directors who have power to refuse to register the transfer to a person of whom they do not approve.

Instead of shares, the word 'stock' is sometimes used. Ordinary stock means the same thing as ordinary shares; do not confuse this with loan stock, which means a loan on fixed interest terms.

There are various kinds of share capital. The ordinary shares usually control the company with one vote per share but there are sometimes different classes of ordinary share with different voting rights. Often special shares are called 'A' shares. These could have no votes at all or they could have ten times as many as the rest of the shares. It is up to the shareholders to decide what rights attach to a new issue of shares.

THE XYZ COMPANY LTD

Balance sheet at 30th June

Last year £		Original cost £	Accumulated depreciation £	This year Net book value £
	Fixed assets			
30400	Equipment	34000	7000	27000
9000	Fixtures and fittings	10000	2000	8000
12000	Vehicles	16000	8000	8000
51400		60000	17000	43000
–	*Patents and trademarks*			10000
3000	*Goodwill*			3000
17000	*Investment in associated company*			17000
	Current assets			
50000	Stocks (trade £65000; other £3000)		68000	
9000	Accounts receivable (debtors)		10000	
2600	Payments in advance		3000	
61600				81000
133000	*Total assets*			154000
	Less			
	Current liabilities			
12000	Accounts payable (creditors)		13000	
9000	Current tax payable		8000	
3500	Ordinary dividend due (final only)		4000	
23500	Bank overdraft		30000	
48000				55000
11000	*Deferred taxation*			15000
10000	*Long-term loan*			10000
£64000	*Shareholders' interest in the business*			£74000
	Represented by:			
	Share capital and reserves			
15000	Ordinary shares of £1 (authorised £20000)			15000
10000	10% preference shares of £1			10000
10000	Capital reserve			10000
29000	Balance of undistributed profit			39000
£64000				£74000

The significance of voting rights is that, ultimately, he who controls over 50 per cent of the votes, controls the company and can appoint the directors. For complete control, over 90 per cent of the votes is needed. The Companies Acts lay down different percentages which are needed to do different things such as change voting rights, repay share capital, etc, but 51 per cent gives control of the day-to-day management of the business.

What is authorised capital?

Shares can be issued at any time in return for money or for an asset acquired by the company up to the limit of its authorised capital. Once the authorised limit has been reached, only the shareholders can approve an increase in it. Any such increase then remains available for issue as required. Thus, in the example, the company has an authorised capital of £20,000 but has only issued £15,000 of it.

Spare capital is not cash

This is not to say that the company has £5000 spare cash. When they authorise a given figure of share capital, the shareholders merely fix a limit upon the powers of the directors. No value is received by the company until it actually issues the shares.

Preference shares £10,000

Preference shares are entitled only to a fixed percentage dividend — ten per cent in the example (based on their nominal value not on the value quoted on the Stock Exchange or elsewhere). The dividend is only payable if the directors consider that the profits (and cash position) are adequate but it ranks in priority before any dividend on the ordinary shares. Normally preference shares have no votes but often they obtain them if their dividend is not paid and this can result in the control of the company changing hands, depending upon the respective voting rights of the ordinary and preference shares.

Some preference dividends are cumulative until all arrears are cleared. Others are non-cumulative and the dividends are lost if not paid for any year.

If the company is wound up, the preference shares rank before the ordinary shares for repayment up to their nominal value. They can, however, be repaid without winding up the company if a majority of the holders agree; the ordinary shares, on the other hand, can only be repaid if the company is either wound up or reconstructed, which is a complicated legal process.

What does 'nominal value' of loan stock and ordinary shares mean?

The nominal value of loan stock or of ordinary shares is the figure which appears in the balance sheet of the issuing company and represents the amount it owes to the holders. In the case of loan stock or preference shares, this is the amount repayable as and when the stock is redeemed or the shares are repaid.

In the case of ordinary shares, however, nominal value is merely the original value set for the shares. Since the ordinary shareholders are entitled to all the profits (and bear any losses) remaining after paying all fixed interest and preference dividends, it follows that should the company be sold or wound up, the ordinary shareholders receive the net proceeds remaining after meeting all other obligations. This may be greater or less than the nominal value of their shares, depending on whether the company has made a profit or loss since the shares were issued.

What is the actual value of shares?

Equally, the nominal value of shares, both ordinary and preference, and of loan stock, has little bearing on their value if sold by one investor to another. The price obtainable, whether on the Stock Exchange or elsewhere, depends upon investors' expectations as to the income obtainable, the security of it, the possibility, for ordinary shares, of its increasing in the future and their assessment of the investment in comparison with the rates of return available elsewhere. The same applies if you sell the entire share capital except, of course, that you are then selling a job as well as an investment.

If a shareholding is large enough to justify a directorship for the holder, this increases its value, particularly in the case of a private company. In fact, the holder of 51 per cent of the shares of the private company can often largely ignore the wishes of the minority holders and in consequence, the latters' shares may be very difficult to sell at anything near the value per share of the majority holding.

Can a small company raise money by issuing shares?

In theory yes. A small company can issue shares to outsiders, but in practice only people closely associated with the proprietor of such a company are likely to agree to back him. It is also illegal to issue a prospectus to the public at large asking them to subscribe for shares, unless you first comply with certain rules. This source of finance is not open to the smaller business in most cases because of the very high risks involved. It is one thing to put money into your own business, but quite another to entrust it to another man to use in his.

Reserves — capital £10,000; profit and loss £39,000

A capital reserve cannot be distributed by way of dividend. It normally arises from a profit on the sale of a capital asset, such as property.

A profit and loss, or revenue reserve, is available for distribution. In fact, it represents the balance of profits earned in previous years but not distributed. Often it is really the additional funds needed to let the company grow, and it represents permanent capital. The cash is not available to pay out.

Having explained the items which make up the shareholders' interest, we now go back to the example on page 30.

Fixed assets £60,000-£17,000 = £43,000

The Companies Act requires the original cost of the assets to be shown. This is therefore the first column in the example. The second column shows the accumulated depreciation written off to date for each year in which the assets have been owned. The third column shows the net book value of £43,000.

These totals cannot of course show any additions or sales during the year and the total values of any such changes have to be given in a separate note to the accounts. Equally the accumulated depreciation figure includes the charge for the year shown in the profit and loss account.

Depreciation for a limited company is usually charged on the 'straight line' basis. Thus, a charge of 25 per cent on the original cost will write off an item over four years. This is in contrast to, say, 33⅓ per cent on the reducing balance, which, although a higher percentage, never completely writes it off, as explained in the previous section.

To use the straight line method accurately, the detailed records of the company must show the total additions separately for each year so that after, say, ten years at ten per cent, the additions for 1969 are no longer depreciated in 1979. Provided that one knows when an item was bought, it is then easy to calculate how much depreciation has been charged by the year in which it is sold, or scrapped. Even if the original cost is not known, it can be estimated and the totals for original cost and accumulated depreciation adjusted to reflect the sale. Without such figures year by year, one cannot tell how much of the assets is fully written off.

If an item has been sold, the difference between the net book value and the price obtained will be shown in the profit and loss account as a profit (or loss) on sale of fixed assets. If the item has been scrapped, the whole of the net book value is a loss unless, of course, it was already fully depreciated and therefore in the books at a net value of nil. The most frequent such figure is the profit or loss on the sale of a motor vehicle.

Plant registers

Vehicles are easy to keep track of but individual machines and equipment can become merged as part of general plant, particularly if moved about. Many companies therefore number plant and keep a plant register so as to identify individual items as to age, specification, cost, etc.

Patents and trade-marks

The XYZ Company Ltd has acquired some patents and trade-marks during the last year. The £10,000 cost could either be the purchase price or the expenses incurred if the company has designed and registered its own patent or mark.

Investment in associated company £17,000

An associated company is one in which the investing company effectively has a say in the management policy and has a director on the other company's board either because it is a partner or because it owns at least 20 per cent of the shares.

Since the investing company can influence the dividends paid to it, the investment is distinguished as 'associated' rather than 'trade'. Both 'associated' and 'trade' investments are held for the longer term but shares can also be held as a short-term home for spare funds, in which case they are treated as a current asset rather than separated, as here.

The investment in an associated company might include the cost of buying shares in it or long-term loans made to it. Any sums due from it for ordinary sales to it, or payable to it for ordinary purchases from it, on normal trade terms, are shown as 'amounts due from (or to) associated companies' in current assets or current liabilities. Note that, under company law, such sums 'in the family' must not be hidden away in ordinary debtors or creditors.

Investments in subsidiary companies

A subsidiary company is one in which your company owns more than half the shares. It therefore controls it for practical purposes. There is no such investment in the example. Companies invest in other companies for many reasons, such as to diversify activities by starting new ones or buying existing operations, to defend themselves against their competitors or to form an alliance with suppliers or customers.

Goodwill was explained in Section 4.

More about stocks

For the retailer or the wholesaler, stocks consist of what is bought in to sell out again in the same state, or with minor changes, such as making up fabric into curtains. Other types of business, particularly manufacturers, often have various kinds of stock such as:

- raw materials
- bought-in parts and sub-assemblies
- work in progress
- finished goods
- stationery, advertising and sales promotion materials, fuel, etc.

These are explained below.

Raw materials

One man's finished goods are another man's raw materials. Raw materials are those goods which a business buys in order to transform them by its production processes into finished products. Examples are the timber, nails, glue, etc bought by a furniture manufacturer or the powders, perfumes and chemicals used by a cosmetics manufacturer.

Bought-in parts

Many businesses buy in parts for use in assembling their products. For instance the cosmetics manufacturer buys in jars and pots in which to put his lotions and creams and the car manufacturer purchases sparking plugs for his engine. Such parts are often distinguished from raw materials by being called bought-in parts, components or even sub-assemblies.

Sub-assemblies are sections of a product put together by a supplier specifically for the manufacturer. A car manufacturer, for instance, might buy in complete door handle and window winding assemblies for his car doors.

Sub-assemblies may also be sections of a product put together by the manufacturer himself and awaiting the next stage in the production process. In this case they will very likely be classified as work in progress.

Work in progress

Work in progress stocks are those which are part-way through the production cycle. For example, a motor vehicle is assembled through various stages. Since the production process is continuous, there are bound to be unfinished vehicles at the date of taking stock.

The term 'work in progress' is also used to describe work done on unfinished construction contracts. In a service industry or a professional office such as that of an accountant or an architect, work in progress is the time spent on jobs which have not yet been charged to the customer or the client because they are incomplete.

The valuation of work in progress should normally be the costs incurred to date, ie materials used plus direct labour costs plus, perhaps, the cost of using machinery, etc in the processes so far carried out and any other costs which can be identified separately to the items concerned. Whether overhead expenses should be included is a matter for individual company policy. Care has to be taken when carrying forward expenses, such as management salaries, rent, telephones, etc as part of the stock valuation, that the total of these overheads included in stock relates to the time taken to produce the goods. Otherwise heavy stocks may mean that too much of the overheads are held over to next year. Since it is the stock figure which is increased, and not the expense figures which are reduced, it is not apparent how much overheads are carried forward unless the figure is calculated separately as part of the valuation.

Finished goods (or, in the USA, 'inventory')

Finished goods are stocks ready for sale to customers. This does not necessarily mean that they are goods which the ultimate customer would recognise. The sub-assembly bought by the car manufacturer for his car door is 'finished goods' to the business which makes it, even though it is several stages away from that at which the car reaches the showroom.

Stationery, advertising and sales promotion materials, heating fuel, etc

These goods are overhead expenses of most businesses rather than part of the direct cost of goods bought or produced for re-sale. Expenditure on them is shown in the profit and loss account as an expense, not as part of cost of sales.

Sales promotional materials are items such as sales brochures, catalogues, sales stands for shop counters, and so on.

38

Once incurred, an expense normally has no residual value, unlike a production cost which produces stock. Often, therefore, stocks of stationery, advertising and sales promotion materials, fuel, etc, are ignored. If the value of such stocks is significant, however, they can be counted and included in the balance sheet. This is often done if a large bill has been incurred just before the end of the financial year for goods which will mostly be used during the following year.

The charge to the expense heading in the profit and loss account is then the total of bills received for the goods in question less the value of the stocks carried forward to the next accounting period (plus any stocks brought forward from the previous accounting period).

Current tax payable £8000

This is the tax due shortly as opposed to the provision for deferred taxation (see below).

Ordinary dividend due £4000

This is the final dividend. The interim dividend was paid during the year as a payment on account. The directors can pay an interim dividend, if they are satisfied that profits will cover it, but the final one needs approval by the shareholders at the annual general meeting.

Deferred taxation £15,000

Current company tax law in the UK allows many companies to postpone the payment of a large part of their tax bills. This is the effective result of allowing them to write off 100 per cent of many (but not all) items of capital expenditure in the year in which tax is incurred. Since the profits declared to the shareholders are after charging part of the cost only, as depreciation, years in which heavy capital expenditure is made show a very small tax bill; the taxable profit, after writing off the expenditure, is much smaller than that shown by the accounts.

In years in which little or no capital expenditure is made, the tax payable will be a high proportion of profit. This is because the accounts will strike a profit after charging depreciation, none of which is allowable for tax because the assets were written off for tax purposes in the year they were bought.

In addition, stock relief now allows a company to reduce its tax bill according to a formula derived from any increase in the value of its stock. The purpose of this is to help it to retain enough cash to finance the very heavy increases in working capital caused by inflation.

In theory this relief is temporary since any reduction in stocks or termination of the business would cause the calculation to be reversed. In practice, stocks tend to go on rising and companies tend to go on spending money on capital assets each year.

As a result, large provisions are being created for deferred taxation in tax equalisation accounts which are supposed to even out the tax bill. In many cases this tax is not likely ever to be paid and meanwhile it is available as long-term capital.

In consequence, many companies now regard these provisions as part of the shareholders' funds, and are only separating as deferred tax the amounts which they expect to have to pay in the foreseeable future.

It should be stressed that the balance of profit left in shareholders' funds, as a result of the lower tax bill, is *not* available for a cash handout to shareholders. It is only there in the first place because the corresponding money has already been spent on equipment or stocks.

Does your company have departmental accounts?

A substantial company may well have a number of different departments or activities. It will want to know how its sales, its expenses and its profits compare for these and its accounts may therefore be in several sections. However many different operating statements there may be in your company, you will see that they build up to a similar overall statement as shown in the earlier example although many of the detailed expenses may be on subsidiary schedules.

Questions on Section 5 *(Check your answers with the text)*

☐ What items does one find in a profit and loss appropriation account?

☐ What governs how much profit a business needs to retain?

☐ What is the meaning of the following:

share capital
authorised capital
preference shares
investments in associated companies?

☐ What kinds of stock are there (five are discussed)?

☐ What is the difference between current and deferred tax?

Section 6:
How Are the Figures in the Profit and Loss Account Arrived at?

The sum shown for each item in the profit and loss account is the amount of income earned or expense incurred during the period. This is a simple idea to grasp in theory, but do you understand what it means in practice? Here are three examples.

Sales

If all your sales are for cash — that is to say, if your customers hand over money (or a cheque) when you give them the goods or service — the total of your sales is the cash received.

But if you allow credit to your customers, is the sales figure:

(a) the total value of the goods and services which you deliver to them in the period (the value of any deliveries not yet invoiced being estimated)?

(b) The total of the invoices which you issue to them in the period?

(c) the total cash you receive from customers in the period?

Purchase of goods for resale

If your suppliers allow you credit, is the value of your purchases:

(a) the value of goods received from suppliers in the period (the value of any deliveries not yet invoiced

being estimated)?
(b) the value of the invoices received from suppliers in
the period?
(c) the total of cash paid to suppliers in the period?

Expenses

An 'expense' is an item of cost incurred in running a
business, such as rent, rates, telephone, etc, as opposed to
goods bought for re-sale to customers.

For example, is the cost of the telephone:

(a) the value of the bills received in the period?
(b) the value of bills received as adjusted by an estimate
for any period not covered by invoices to hand?
(c) the total cash paid to the telephone service?

For both sales and purchases (a) and (b) may be the same
figures but this depends on whether your own and your
suppliers' invoicing is up to date. The longer you wait
before closing your records for the period, the fewer any
missing invoices will be.

Example of how the basic arithmetic works

The sales calculation is:	£
Cash received during the period	10000
Less accounts receivable at start of period (ie debtors — amounts owing to you). These are included in the cash receipts for this period but apply to the last one, so we deduct them.	1000
	9000
Add accounts receivable at the end of the period (the reverse of the above)	800
Sales for period	£9800

The purchases calculation is the same but uses the totals of
money paid out and accounts payable (creditors — amounts
owing by you) at the start and the end of the period.

This produces a figure for goods for resale bought in the
period. If you refer to the example of a profit and loss

account, you will see how the purchases total is then adjusted by opening and closing stocks to give the cost of goods sold.

The above questions concerning sales, purchases and expenses demonstrate that the figures relating to the period covered by a profit and loss account are not necessarily just the cash you have paid or the invoices you have issued or received. Often these figures need adjusting to make them show the full story, not just those bits of it which happen to have been recorded so far.

The correct answers to the examples are (a), (a) and (b). Do you understand why?

It is a common mistake to think of money as being spent when the payment is made: in fact, this is often just the settlement of a debt which may have been incurred much earlier.

The bank account shows the money coming in and the money going out, but this is no guide to the profit. To show the true position, we must allow for sales and liabilities for which we have not yet received the cash or for which we have not yet paid.

When is a sale a sale?

If you sell services, it is the date of the invoice to the customer which determines the accounting period into which the sale goes. All services provided up to the end of each period must either be invoiced or their value to date estimated as 'work in progress'. If you sell goods, the sale is made when they are delivered to the customer (or when you invoice him for a progress payment, if this applies).

Watch your 'cut off' of goods against invoice

If you sell goods on credit, you must tie up the despatch of the goods with the invoices you issue. You would be taking a double profit if the goods were to be counted in stock and invoices for them also included in the sales. All goods which are despatched by the end of the accounting period must therefore be invoiced and included in your total of accounts receivable (debtors); conversely, goods still held are counted as stock and the invoice is dated in the following period in which they are actually despatched.

This procedure is sometimes called the 'cut off' because it determines the point at which your stop invoicing for one period and start for the next. The same procedure works in reverse for purchases of goods for resale (see below).

When is a purchase a purchase?

On the payments side the biggest problem is usually the receipt of goods bought from suppliers. Goods received before stock-taking will be included in the value of stocks counted, therefore the corresponding liability to the supplier must be included in accounts payable (creditors).

On the other hand, we do not want to include any suppliers' invoices in accounts payable unless the goods have been counted in stock.

This can only be done accurately if the suppliers' delivery notes are marked with the dates of receipt of the goods. Subsequently, these documents are tied up with the invoices received from suppliers.

Conversely, the date of receipt of any goods received after stock-taking should be marked on the delivery notes so as to prevent the invoices being included in accounts payable. The invoices belong to the following accounting period because the goods have not been counted in stock. It is sometimes necessary to estimate the value of invoices outstanding at the end of the accounting period in cases where suppliers are very slow to invoice.

This procedure for ensuring that invoices for goods bought are charged to the correct accounting period is especially important because the sums of money involved are often large in relation to other figures in the accounts. If the 'cut off' is wrong the profit margin percentage may well be seriously incorrect. If this is not realised, the accounts may be misleading and cause wrong decisions to be taken.

Example

The stocks include goods received just before stock-taking to the value of £1000, for which no corresponding invoice is included in accounts payable. As a result, the cost of goods sold is reduced and the profit is increased.

If sales are £50,000, an extra £1000 profit is two per cent. If this makes the gross profit margin appear in the accounts as 20 per cent when the real figure is 18 per cent an owner who expected say 21 per cent, could then be misled. He might well accept a one per cent drop when he ought to be investigating one of three per cent.

Expenses

In the case of services bought in such as electricity, telephone, etc it is also often necessary to estimate the amount due for the period from the date of the last invoice received to the end of the accounting period.

Deposits received in advance

Some businesses take deposits or payments in advance from customers. Where money has been received in advance of the services being performed or the goods supplied, the amounts outstanding must be listed and carried forward as payments in advance from customers. Otherwise the profits will be inflated and too much tax may be payable, quite apart from the accounts failing to show a fair view of the position.

To summarise the objective of the profit and loss account

The objective of the profit and loss account is to show the profits earned during the period from the sales made to customers and to charge the correct expenses both for goods 'used up' in supplies to customers and for services consumed in running the business during the period. This is done regardless of whether invoices have been paid, or received.

It is whether or not a liability has been incurred which decides whether a cost is a charge against the profit. The actual payment, in cash or by cheque, is merely the settlement of that liability.

Questions on Section 6
☐ Return to the first page of this section and revise the question there.

Section 7:
Points on Public Company Accounts

This section is mainly for those who work for or have to understand the accounts of public companies or of groups of companies.

What do the published accounts of a company show?

The Companies Acts do not require a detailed profit and loss account to be issued to shareholders or to be filed at Companies House. Your company's annual report may well be an expensive glossy production, but you will find that it does not show very much detailed information about sales and expenses when compared with internal management accounts. The latter contain confidential details which do not have to be made public.

The published accounts only give the sales and certain expenses such as directors' salaries, interest and the audit fee in the profit and loss account. They do not show the cost of sales or the detail of other costs, though they do give information on wages.

The balance sheet details are much more comprehensive and probably correspond very closely to your internal accounts.

What are 'shareholders' and 'directors'?

The shareholders provide money to finance the business. This is called share capital and is explained in more detail later. They hand over cash or assets and receive shares in the company in exchange.

The board of directors runs the business. Individual directors may or may not own shares in it. In small businesses, the directors and shareholders are often the same people. Equally the directors of a small company usually work full-time in it.

A *'non-executive' director,* however, is not a manager working full-time; he merely attends board meetings. He is really a consultant or adviser and his fees are often much smaller than those of the full-time director.

Who controls the company — directors or shareholders?

The directors run the company and take the decisions. However, they have to obtain the approval of the shareholders for certain actions, changes in the share capital for instance, and they have to present accounts each year. Ultimately, the shareholders can tell the directors what to do. They cannot run the company themselves, so this really means that they can vote new directors onto the board, whom they think will run the business more to their liking than did the old ones.

This is an important legal point in large companies whose directors often hold a very small proportion of the shares. In practice the directors do not often get voted out by the shareholders unless they have run the business very badly or unless their conduct has been highly controversial and public opinion has been aroused.

Who are shareholders nowadays?

Nowadays the people who provide the money for companies to expand are more likely to be pension funds, unit trusts and similar large institutions rather than private individuals. The really big sums are channelled through these institutions whether as company pension schemes or as private insurance policies, and inherited individual wealth is less and less a source of share capital.

49

Why are dividends paid to shareholders?

The ordinary shareholders take the biggest risk. They are
the first to suffer if things go wrong and, should the
company go out of business, they are the last to be paid
after all the other creditors and lenders to the company. In
return for their risk, they are entitled to all the surplus,
should profits be made. In practice they cannot take all
this out of the company both for tax reasons and because
the business needs retained profit. Just as you expect
interest on your savings in a building society or bank
deposit account, the shareholder needs an income from his
much higher risk investment. He does not always get it. He
only receives dividends provided that there is enough *cash*
to spare, not just profit. He is taxed on these dividends as
unearned private income.

If the directors are also the shareholders, they will prefer to
take their share of profits as earned salaries rather than
unearned dividends. Sometimes a director, who is a major
shareholder, waives his right to a dividend thus allowing
other shareholders, who are not directors, to receive an
income whilst leaving more cash in the company.

Is a dividend of £7000 on share capital £15,000 big money'?

This is the figure from the example in the last section. But
it is not what it seems. This comparison is with the
nominal value of the shares which is the amount originally
invested by the shareholders. This may have been many
years ago in which case the profits retained in the company
each year will have built up to substantial sums. These
reserves are often as much as or even substantially greater
than the nominal share capital.

The successful investment of these accumulated reserves
will have increased the annual profit. The dividend will
therefore have risen as well. If you re-calculate it at as a
percentage of the total shareholders' funds including
reserves, you will find that it is much lower and that in
many cases it represents no more than a modest return to

the investor on his true investment. Here the shareholders' interest is £74000 (see balance sheet) so the return is under ten per cent; the dividends are taxed as unearned income in the shareholders' hands anyway.

In the case of a quoted company the Stock Exchange price for the shares may or may not be close to their value as shown by the balance sheet, depending upon the popularity or otherwise of the shares. The return to the investor is his dividend as a percentage of the price of his shares and it can be as low as two to three per cent even in a depressed share market. Only if there is serious doubt about the company's future profits will the dividend yield go much above ten per cent. So high nominal dividends are not what they seem.

Nowadays many companies express their dividends in pence per share because dividend restraint has meant that they have to calculate to many decimal places the maximum which they are allowed to pay. The principle, however, is the same.

Dividend 'cover'

In some sets of accounts, the accumulated balance on the profit and loss account is added to the profit after tax before showing the dividends paid. This has the effect of hiding the key point of dividend 'cover', ie how much is paid out in dividends compared with the amount of profit retained.

In the example the cover is £17,000(after the preference dividend) for £7000 or about 2.4 times.

Consolidated balance sheets

If a company has one or more subsidiaries (or 'associated' companies), they form a group of companies. None of the balance sheets of the individual companies will show the total value of the group. In the example previously explained, the holding company shows only the value of its investment in its subsidiaries or associates at cost. This may not reflect the real value, particularly if the investment was made some years ago.

For this reason a consolidated balance sheet is prepared for groups of companies, which shows the overall position of the group. It adds together all the assets and liabilities of the individual companies as shown by their respective balance sheets.

Naturally the inter-company balances have to be cancelled against each other. This is quite simple since each amount is an asset in one balance sheet and a liability in the other.

The share capital of each subsidiary cancels against the investment in that subsidiary shown as a parent company asset. If the subsidiary is not fully owned, the consolidated balance sheet will show as a liability, the minority interest representing the shares not owned. If the parent company paid more for its investment than the nominal value of the shares, the premium is shown as goodwill in the consolidated balance sheet.

This is a simplified explanation of how a consolidated balance sheet is prepared. To look at, it is much the same as an ordinary balance sheet, the main difference being that if any subsidiaries are not fully owned or if an associate company's figures are consolidated the value of the outsiders' share of the group assets will be shown under the heading 'minority interest'.

What matters to creditors or lenders?

Since the consolidated balance sheet shows the overall position it tends to be given prominence and the parent company's balance sheet is often ignored by readers of accounts. However, this can be a mistake if you are a creditor or are lending money either to the parent company or to one of its subsidiaries.

The group, as consolidated, has no legal existence. It is individual companies whom one must sue in any dispute and, unless guarantees have been given, they are not responsible for each other's debts. It is usually impossible, legally speaking, to force a parent company to make good a deficiency in the assets of one of its subsidiaries.

It might be possible to realise the assets of a wholly owned subsidiary if you could force the parent into liquidation but it could be a long business if the subsidiary's directors were independent and reluctant to co-operate.

Remember that 51 per cent of a company is not enough to force a liquidation against the wishes of the other shareholders. Many consolidated balance sheets also include the assets of associate companies of which less than half the shares are owned. The creditors of the holding company are probably powerless to realise the assets of an associate company. Almost certainly their only possible course is to sell the shares and it might be very difficult to find a buyer for these unless they are quoted on the Stock Exchange.

So, whilst consolidated balance sheets give vital information about the overall picture, they can be very misleading if used to assess the security for a loan or an ordinary trading debt.

Look also at the parent company's figures (the holding company's balance sheet is published as well as the consolidated figures) or at those of the particular subsidiary with which you deal. Enquire for a parent company guarantee if in doubt.

What about income from associated companies?

If company A owns less than 50 per cent of company B, B is not a subsidiary but is often treated in the balance sheet of company A as an associated company, as explained in the previous section.

The significance of the 'associated company' heading is that the share of B's profits, which relates to the shares in it which A owns, is then brought in to A's consolidated accounts. This is in contrast to treating the income as being

53

merely the actual dividend received.

One result of this is to show the group income as much larger than the amount over which the parent company's directors have direct control. They may not be able to force payment of a larger share of their associated company's profits and their own reported income may overstate the security available to a lender or creditor.

There is often a big difference between the dividend paid and the total profit applicable to a shareholding. This will depend upon the policy of the paying company, how much it needs to retain to pay for expansion plans, and so on.

There have been many cases of companies holding valuable investments in other companies which were shown at a fraction of their true value, both because this was stated at a historic cost often many years old, and because the income shown ignored the profits retained by the paying company. Often it was very difficult for outsiders to appreciate the facts for lack of detailed information. On the Stock Exchange this led to some unsatisfactory situations in which companies were taken over for prices vastly greater than their shares had been valued at on the basis of the published information available immediately before the take-over bid. The associated company method of accounting was therefore adopted in order to reflect the true position more closely.

Net assets per share

This is a figure often quoted in the financial press in connection with public companies. In the example, the calculation is:

	£
Shareholders' interest	74000
Less preference shares	10000
	£64000
Divide by 15,000 = per share	£4.27

Questions on Section 7 (Check your answers with the text)
- ☐ What is the difference between a shareholder and a director?
- ☐ Why do shareholders need dividends?
- ☐ What is dividend cover?
- ☐ What is the difference between the balance sheet of a parent company and that of the whole group (ie the consolidated balance sheet)?

Section 8:
A Bit More about the Balance Sheet — Some More Terms

Note: The figures in this section use the balance sheet in Section 4, not that in Section 5.

Capital employed

The total funds in use by the business, ie the total of its assets. In the example this is £15,400

Net capital employed

Total assets less current liabilities, except the bank overdraft. Current liabilities, principally creditors, are in effect finance provided by outsiders for short periods. Thus the net capital which the owner has to provide is reduced by the normal trade credit he receives. The overdraft, in contrast, is a method of financing part of his cash needs and does not arise automatically from trading. Therefore it should not reduce the net capital employed figure which in the example is £15,400-£2800 = £12,600 .

An important measure of the profitability of the business is the return earned upon net capital employed. See under balance sheet ratios.

Working capital

The cash required to operate the business from day to day, ie to pay for stocks, debtors, advance payments to creditors, deposits, etc, less creditors, advance payment from customers, etc. Thus current assets less current liabilities represents at the date of the balance sheet the working capital in use by the business. Any bank overdraft should be added back to the net balance since this represents a temporary loan to provide working capital which is subject to withdrawal. It is more realistic to regard it as a means of funding than as part of working capital.

Net capital employed and working capital

The respective figures from the example are set out to show how the two terms differ.

	Net capital Employed £	Working capital £
Fixed assets and goodwill	7300	N/A
Current assets	8100	8100
	15400	8100
Less current liabilities except bank overdraft	2800	2800
Net Capital Employed/ Working Capital	£12600	£5300
Funded by:		
the bank	3000	3000
the owner	8600	2300
long-term loan	1000	N/A
	£12600	£5300

In this case the bank is providing 57 per cent of the net working capital, which is all right but the bank might not wish the proportion to go higher. See also under balance sheet ratios.

Too high a proportion of bank finance is often a sign of overtrading. This means expanding sales beyond the capacity of the business to provide the necessary working capital for stock and debtors — hence increased borrowings.

Questions on Section 8 (*Check your answers with the text*)

What is:
☐ capital employed?
☐ net capital employed?
☐ working capital?

Section 9:
What Does the Profit and Loss Account Tell Me?

Your accounts tell a story

Individual figures in your accounts mean little. It is in comparison with other figures that the key facts emerge.

Assessing your profits

Your profit and loss account shows you the result of your trading. Is it satisfactory?

Sales — did you sell more?

How much was the sales increase last year? Did it keep pace with inflation in the price of the goods or services you sell or did a rise in money totals, resulting from higher prices, conceal a fall in the volume of business?

Sales — how much could you have sold?

Is there a limit to your possible sales and if so, how close did you get? If you are providing a service, you are really selling time. There may be skills and/or materials involved as well but it is time you are selling and there is only so much of it, unless you take on more staff. Once a service has sold enough hours to cover its fixed costs, every extra hour sold is profit subject only to materials and any other direct expenses. So a key factor in the profitability of a service is how close it gets to selling all its available time. On the other hand, once it is near to its maximum potential, it may only be able to increase sales by raising prices.

Even a business selling goods may have an effective limit to its market. A shop on a housing estate normally can only hope to sell to people living on the estate. Their expenditure on any particular line of goods will be limited and the shop cannot hope for business beyond that limit.

How close are you to the effective limits to your volume of sales?

Are you making the right gross profit?

In the earlier section on the profit and loss account, we mentioned gross profit. Of all the key figures, this is the least understood and we therefore devote more space here to this very important subject.

This is what 'gross profit' means

Suppose you are a shopkeeper selling cakes at £2 each, which you buy at £1.50. You make a profit of 50p which is 25 per cent of the selling price. For simplicity, let us assume this is all you sell.

If you dispose of 200 cakes a week, your gross profit is 25 per cent on sales of 200 x £2 = £400, ie £100 or 50p per cake. If the fixed costs of running your shop are £90 per week, you have a net profit of £10, or 5p per cake.

What happens to net profit if you raise your sales to 300 cakes per week? Stop here for a moment and work out for yourself, before reading on, how much your gross profit is and the net profit per cake.

300 cakes = sales £600 at 25 per cent = gross profit £150 (50p per cake) less fixed costs £90 = net profit £60 or 20p per cake. Your sales are up by half, gross profit per cake has remained unchanged but net profit per cake has multiplied four times from 5p to 20p and the amount of net profit six times from £10 to £60.

The reason of course is that the fixed costs (wages, rent,

rates, electricity, etc,) remain the same whether you sell one cake or 300. Perhaps a higher volume of sales creates a few more telephone calls or a little more wear and tear on fittings and equipment but such extra costs are insignificant. Of course, wages will rise when your existing staff can no longer cope but this will be a major jump due to extra staff being taken on and will relate directly to the number of people you employ, not to the volume of sales as such, even though the latter is the cause.

Once you have paid your fixed costs, each extra cake sold produces 50p more net profit and that net profit spread over all the cakes sold rises dramatically (until you have to engage extra staff).

Some cakes are wasted

Sadly, life is not so simple that that is the end of the story. Not every cake you buy gets sold. Here is why:

— Some get pushed to the back during busy sales periods and fresh stock goes in front by mistake, so the other ones go past their 'sell by' dates and have to be eaten by the owner or given to staff.

— A few just fail to sell — the fillings, sizes, etc are not quite what customers want that week.

— Other cakes are spoilt in the window when the sun comes out unexpectedly and staff are too busy to erect the blind.

— Occasionally you guess the demand completely wrong: the weather alters unexpectedly, there is a local scare about hygiene, another shop is prosecuted for selling cream cakes which are not fresh, or some similar event temporarily cuts sales and you find you have overbought.

— You deliver a large order to a local caterer and include an extra cake in error. You price your invoice to him incorrectly or calculate the total wrongly.

— Your supplier short delivers you and you fail to check in time. Alternatively he overcharges you per cake or makes a calculating error on his invoice which you do not spot. Occasionally he delivers the wrong cakes, too many cakes or substandard cakes and you do not discover these errors (deliberate or genuine) in time to claim credit.

— You are busy when your supplier delivers and you do not notice the van driver removing one of the cartons which you have just hurriedly signed for. (He sells it for cash elsewhere.)

— One of your sales girls gives special prices to her friends without your knowledge, or permission. A second assistant gets into financial trouble and starts to 'borrow' from the till. Another assistant has a sweet tooth and either eats on the premises or takes home cakes which are still fresh and in date, and customers pilfer a proportion of your stock.

— Your store room is crowded and you trip over a carton squashing it and sending another flying, rendering cakes unsaleable in both cartons.

— Your competitor down the road finds a new source of cheaper supplies and he cuts prices, forcing you to follow suit.

— Some of your cakes sell by weight and there are minor but consistent undercharges to customers. Others are priced too low by mistake.

We hope your shop is not subject to such a catalogue of calamities all at once but there is no shop, or any other business, which is free from all of them. Whatever your trade or industry, similar problems arise.

The results of poor control of gross profit

Suppose that all the losses add up to one per cent of the cakes you sell, ie three cakes on 300, value £6 at sale prices. Your figures are then:

Sales: 297 at £2	594
Cost of goods sold: 300 at £1.50	450
Gross profit	144
Net profit	54

ie a reduction of ten per cent from the previous profit of £60.

This level of loss may not seem too bad: but what if the losses are three per cent — nine cakes = £18 sales. The net profit is then down from £60 to £42, a fall of 30 per cent. That is quite a cut in your personal pay packet! And the dreadful thing is that three per cent of sales is on the low side for many businesses for pilferage losses, let alone all the others. Since many make less than ten per cent of sales as net profit, you can see how serious this is.

Your gross profit is vital!

In the example of a profit and loss account in Section 3, gross profit (GP) has fallen from 24½ to 23 per cent. 1½ per cent on sales of £47,500 is £700. On the net profit of £4700 this is 15 per cent. But one ought to compare it with the 'super' profit of £1700 on which it is 41 per cent.

Small variations in GP often have a major impact upon the real profitability of the business. Usually it is easier to save one per cent of GP on sales than it is ten per cent of an expense item. In the example given one per cent on sales is £475 which dwarfs the likely savings resulting from a blitz on expenses.

In retailing, similar shops start with roughly the same gross profit to play with. One supermarket's margins will be similar to another's; a small grocer buys on similar terms to other small grocers. As fixed expenses for equivalent shops are also similar, the main reason for the big differences in the net profit earned by comparable businesses is control of gross profit.

In non-retail businesses, other factors may play a bigger part but it is *always* true that the most effective way to raise profits is to tackle gross profit, because this is the largest figure which is susceptible to profit improvement.

Boosting sales is *not* an alternative; it is merely one way of increasing gross profit. Higher sales at lower prices do not necessarily mean more gross profit. Improving your cost of sales by better purchasing, more efficient use of materials or labour also means the same thing — more gross profit.

Factors which affect gross profit

Here are some of the factors:

(a) Wastage of all kinds: many of the causes have already been mentioned.

(b) Pricing policy — low price/high volume or high price/low volume/discounts offered.

(c) Skill in buying the right goods at the right price and in the right quantities.

(d) Cash discounts obtained for prompt payment.

(e) Manufacturing efficiency (if applicable), ie
  (i) effective use of materials
  (ii) minimal machine down time
  (iii) best use of production labour/efficient scheduling
  (iv) quality control.

(f) Time charge out ratios (for service industries and the professions)
  (i) maximum hours charged out in ratio to those available from owners and staff
  (ii) control of work on own administration or equipment
  (iii) control of sickness/absenteeism etc.

There are three important accounting points on which errors affect the gross profit shown in the accounts.

(1) The stock valuation. Obviously, if you have not counted and valued your stocks accurately at the prices you paid, your gross profit will be distorted.

(2) Outstanding bills. Your purchases figure, which is part of the cost of sales calculation, cannot be

correct if you have not included all the invoices outstanding for goods you have used or counted in stock.

(3) Sales on credit. All deliveries to customers, made prior to stock-taking, must be invoiced if the sales figure is to be correct.

Analyse your gross profit

If your business sells different goods at widely differing profit margins, it pays to analyse your gross profit because an average will be meaningless. For example, a public house may have the following sales:

	Gross profit %	Sales £	Gross profit £
Bar	35%	10000	3500
Wines	60%	3000	1800
Food	60%	8000	4800
Accommodation	N/A	5000	5000
	Average 58.1%	£26000	£15100

The *average* gross profit percentage, 58.1 per cent, is useless as a ratio for judging the results of the pub. It is made up of margins which vary widely and it is merely a statistic resulting from that particular sales mix. In order to assess the figures, it is necessary to look at them broken down by section of the business.

To illustrate this, suppose that the barman stole £20 per week, (£1000 pa). In analysed accounts this would show up as a hole in the bar gross profit which would drop to only 27.8 per cent; ie £2500 on £9000. It would be evident that something was wrong.

If the figures were not analysed, the theft would reduce the overall gross profit to 56.4 per cent; ie £14,100 on £25,000 How could one spot the problem? Most likely it would go undetected because there would be no easy way of calculating what the gross profit ought to be.

So if your gross profits on different items vary widely, make sure you split your sales somehow. Even if you have to estimate the split using purchases grossed up by assumed profit margins, this is better than nothing.

Wages and salaries

The importance of staff costs obviously varies with the type of business. In service industries, repair workshops and catering for example it tends to be vital because sales often depend upon the efficiency of staff use. Thus a cafe at peak periods can only improve its sales if customers are served more quickly and it is more susceptible than other businesses to loss of sales because it is full.

Where labour itself is being sold, as in a repair workshop, the number of hours charged to customers, as a percentage of those paid for to staff, is a key ratio. Overtime hours worked may well be another.

Staff costs are important also because, after cost of sales, they are usually the largest expense and therefore offer the most scope for economy. It is good practice to put them at the top of the expenses list for this reason. Many sets of accounts hide the facts on staff costs by splitting them up under different headings; such analysis is often meaningless and merely conceals the size of this important figure.

Care should be taken to group all staff costs together. Pension contributions, travel costs and car expenses are examples of items which are just as much a cost of employing people as their actual wages. They should be shown as separate totals if significant but grouped together.

Other expenses

In some trades advertising and sales promotion costs such as catalogues, brochures, etc are major items.

The rest of your expenses are unlikely to matter very much. You must be aware of them but many, such as rent and rates, can only be altered by moving premises. Few, if any, will be big enough to matter as much as gross profit and wages.

Concentrate on your key figures

In most businesses there are only two or three figures which have a major impact on profits and which also change daily or weekly. They are usually sales, gross profit margins, wages (or staff use) and perhaps one other, depending on the business. These four items have a far greater impact than all the other details put together.

Go through your detailed costs once or twice a year to see if you can cut out items, stop using this or that service, simplify equipment such as telephones, improve heating efficiency, etc. Then leave them alone and concentrate on the things you can change day by day, where improvements can yield really big benefits.

Figures as a percentage of sales

Since only the gross profit varies directly with sales, this is the most useful profit and loss ratio.

Staff costs as a percentage of annual sales over a period of years may be significant because it can reveal trends. To control staff costs, however, one must refer to numbers employed, pay rises negotiated, etc.

Other expenses

In some cases advertising and promotion is a big cost which requires highlighting as a percentage of sales, because average industry ratios are a useful comparison with the competition.

Most of the other expenses of a business are either not big enough in relation to GP and wages to matter, or are fixed. Other expenses therefore are not usually key ratios.

Net profit percentage on sales

This is a useful guide to progress of a business over a period of years. Sometimes it is a valid comparison between businesses in the same trade. However, its value is as a relative figure in comparison with others. Absolute percentage profits on sales vary enormously. Even in the same trade, different businesses may have quite different methods of operation. One may process customers' materials whilst another supplies its own. The sales totals will be very different to achieve the same net profit.

Net profit expressed as return on net capital employed is a key ratio which is dealt with under balance sheet key ratios.

Do not misuse ratios

Refer back to the net profits per cake quoted earlier. The rise from 5p to 20p per cake was interesting, exciting, big news. But what did it actually tell you about the business other than that profits were improving fast? Nothing, because the ratio, as a basis for management action, is meaningless and is of interest only as an annual trend indicator. Many people who ought to know better waste their own and others' time on ratios which are either meaningless or misleading in terms of day-to-day management.

Some managers (some accountants too) regard ratios as an end in themselves, regardless of what useful action may result. They insist on calculating them and they use the figures which are readily available, whether or not these are comparable or relevant, and without troubling to ask themselves why. The effect on the morale of their subordinates or colleagues who know the results to be useless but who are expected to respond to or explain them, can be disastrous. Might you be guilty?

Questions on Section 9 (*Check your answers with the text*)
□ Which are the key ratios in the example given and discussed above?
□ Which are the key ratios in your own business?
□ Why are they relevant and why do they matter?

Section 10:
What Does the Balance Sheet Tell Me?

Are the figures typical?

The balance sheet only gives figures at one particular date. This may or may not be typical — many financial year ends are at quiet periods to ease stock-taking, etc.

When considering balance sheet ratios, therefore:

(a) consider whether the figures used reflect the normal position.

(b) use the correct figures which relate to each other; thus debtor balances relate to sales immediately prior to the balance sheet date, not to the average for the whole period. Also they include VAT, unlike the sales figure.

Current assets to current liabilities

This is an important test. The correct ratio varies from trade to trade and with the nature of the assets. In retailing one might be happy with anything over 1.25 to 1 because stocks, correctly managed, are fairly easily cleared and are often largely funded by creditors.

In manufacturing stocks have to be held longer and in various stages of production so that one cannot rely as much upon credit. A ratio of at least 1.5 to 1 is desirable.

In the example it is £8100 to £5800 or 1.4 (last year 1.3).

Another factor in judging a particular situation is the extent to which the bank is financing current assets. An overdraft, being repayable upon demand, is not the same as normal trade credit, which will continue so long as the trade reputation of the business is good.

Properly managed businesses keep their current ratios in line. A ratio which is below average for the particular trade is a sign of one or more faults:

(a) losses eroding cash.
(b) bad cash planning — using short-term money to pay for fixed assets or to fund long-term projects.

Whilst an above average current ratio may reflect financial strength, it may also suggest idle cash and a business which is not fully exploiting its resources.

Liquidity — the acid test

This is a more severe test of the ability of the business to pay its debts, sometimes called the 'acid test'. It is the ratio of quick assets — those current assets which can quickly be turned into cash — to current liabilities.

In the example, debtors of £1000 compare with current liabilities of £5800. Stocks do not count as quick assets because, in most cases, only a part of them could be realised quickly. Often that part of stocks which is saleable at once is matched by debtors from whom rapid payment is not obtainable.

The seriousness of the position in the example depends upon when the tax is payable and upon the attitude of the bank. Should it put on pressure for a reduction in the overdraft this could only come from cutting stocks.

In the example, the business has an overdraft. Naturally, if there is cash in the bank, this counts as part of quick assets.

Debtors to sales: expressed in number of days' sales

This is debtors including VAT compared with sales after adding back VAT. The correct ratio is that of debtors to sales for the weeks immediately prior to the date of the balance sheet, *not* debtors to the average of the annual sales. Naturally more detail is required where sales fluctuate in the course of a year than that shown in the profit and loss account.

In the example little credit is given and debtors are a few days' sales only.

The ratio indicates whether a proper credit control policy is in force. The correct number of days outstanding varies of course from trade to trade.

Stocks to usage (cost of sales): expressed in number of days' usage held

Again the stocks at the balance sheet date are often low in comparison with the average so that the ratio requires enquiry before acceptance as valid. Also not all stocks shown necessarily relate to cost of sales. Some may be stationery, fuel or other expense items.

In the example, trade stocks of £6500 against average usage (cost of sales) of £36560 or £703 weekly suggests 9¼ weeks' usage held (last year £570 pw = 8.4 weeks). This might be reasonable for a manufacturer or retailer working on high profit margins, but would be too high for a grocer, for example, whose stocks should be fast-moving because of low margins. But is the June stock figure representative?

In the case of a manufacturer, cost of sales might include some labour and other production costs: so might the stock valuation, and this needs enquiry before accepting the ratio. Labour and other costs must be eliminated from the calculation.

The stocks ratio indicates the effectiveness of the control of buying, skill in forecasting sales, the efficiency of the stockroom and, where applicable, the efficiency in production. It is vitally important. Bad stock control ties up both cash and space. It causes stock losses through damage, excess quantities, etc, and makes it more difficult to bring in new lines, change policy to meet new conditions, etc.

Creditors to purchases and expenses: expressed in number of days' purchases

Recent purchases may not correspond with average usage. As an example, a build-up of stocks for Christmas might invalidate a ratio based on figures at 30 November unless the ratio was calculated by working backwards from that date. Remember that creditors include VAT but purchases do not.

In the example, purchases are £38260 and those expenses incurred on credit about £1600. Adding VAT at eight per cent the total is £43000, or about £830 weekly average. Less than two weeks' credit suggests a failure to use normal trade terms. If prompt payment for cash is being made to obtain cash discounts, why has the gross profit ratio fallen? Or is the June creditors total not representative?

The ratio indicates the extent to which creditors are paid promptly. This has various implications concerning reputation, discounts obtained, etc.

Net profit to net capital employed

In the example, net capital employed is £15400 − £2800 = £12600. Adding back interest on the overdraft and loan of £500 gives a profit of £5200, or 41.3 per cent (last year £4600 on £11900 = 38.7 per cent). This is well ahead of the interest cost on the money borrowed.

Super profit to proprietor's interest

But look at this ratio: super profit of £1700 on owner's interest of £8600 is under 20 per cent. If the calculation is adjusted for interest and loans the figures are £2200 on £12600 = 17.5 per cent (last year £2200 on £11900 = 18.5 per cent). The overdraft might cost as much as this at the worst moments of high interest rates.

The calculation of true profit, ie after charging a working wage for the owner, as a percentage of his interest in the business is often a salutory exercise.

You must aim to earn a premium over the return obtainable

from selling the business, taking a job and investing the cash. Otherwise why bother with the extra effort and responsibility and the longer working hours?

Equally, if expansion is planned, the cash borrowed, or realised from investments, to pay for it must earn a profit in excess of its interest cost.

In the example, the current super profit on net capital employed is 17.5 per cent but this present situation should not necessarily rule out borrowing money at, say, 20 per cent. If, for example, £3000 could be borrowed at 20 per cent for a project which would generate extra sales of £10000 at the same gross profit of 23 per cent without extra staff or other significant expenses, the result would be as follows:

	Super profit before interest £	Net capital employed £	Per-centage return
Current	2200	12600	17.5%
New sales £10000 at 23% GP = extra profit	2300		
Cash borrowed at 20% interest cost	(600)	3000	
New result	£3900	£15600	25.0%

Whilst this example may be a little optimistic in propounding a sales increase of £10000 on £47500 without increasing overheads, it does illustrate how figures need to be seen in perspective, not in isolation.

In this example, the current figures might reflect under-use of assets and staff which is remedied by the new project even though the money costs 20 per cent to borrow. Hence all the extra gross profit comes through as net profit.

Question on Section 10 (*Check your answers with the text*)
☐ What are the seven ratios mentioned above?
☐ In what form is each expressed?

Section 11:
How Cash Circulates
in a Business

Why do cash ratios matter?

Many of the key business ratios previously explained reveal
the efficiency with which cash is used. A business can get
away with bad cash use reflected in poor liquidity, high
debtors, stocks and creditors, heavy overdrafts, etc,
provided its profitability is high. But as soon as anything
goes wrong, its cash shortage puts it at risk. Any loss of
confidence by its creditors squeezes it hard. A business
which is basically profitable but which mismanages its cash
can easily be toppled by a temporary setback into
liquidation because it has no room to manoeuvre.

A basic rule of cash management

Fixed assets and long-term development should be financed
by retained profits or by loans on fixed repayment terms.
That way one can plan for repayment of the cash out of
profits.

Bank overdrafts are only suitable for financing current
assets such as debtors and stock. Being repayable on
demand, they should only be invested in assets which can
be realised quickly. Otherwise you are in the dangerous
position of investing long and borrowing short.

Cash is your lifeblood!

Businesses go bust for lack of cash, not necessarily because
they are not making profits. What actually breaks them is
inability to pay their bills.

The water tank chart

How well does your business use its money? Efficient cash control is vital to stability and profits. Do you realise that your equipment, stocks and amounts owed by customers are 'money' to be controlled, just like your bank balance?

The chart shows, in engineers' language, how these items soak up money. Cash circulates like water which flows through a system of tanks, partly by gravity and partly through a pump.

Where does the money come from?

At the start, the owner(s) provide loans or pay up share capital, the bank may make a loan or provide an overdraft facility. All this finance flows into the bank account.

Gravity feed

From the bank account cash flows out at the turn of a tap into fixed assets and stocks. Some is lost as stock wastage. A little comes back when assets are sold off at the end of their useful life, or when obsolete.

Perhaps less readily, cash is then absorbed in giving credit for sales. Some leaks away as bad debts. How much each tank absorbs depends on how you run your business.

The gross profit margin

The cost in cash of a sale is what you have spent in producing the item or providing the service. You assume a profit on the sale at that time, not when the cash is received, and this is added to the amount owing by the customer which is shown in your balance sheet. This profit inflates the debtors tank, but is not yet cash in hand.

The pump house gets the money back in

From then on cash only flows back up round the system

HOW CASH CIRCULATES IN A BUSINESS

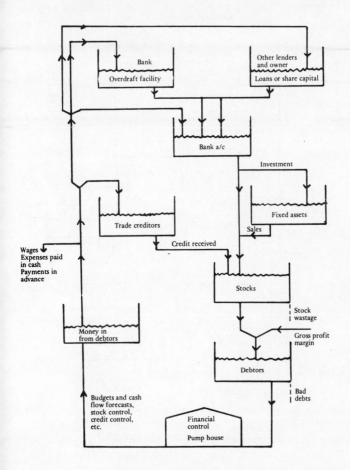

HOW CASH CIRCULATES IN A BUSINESS

Exercise: Fill in descriptions in the correct places. They are listed at the bottom of the Chart.

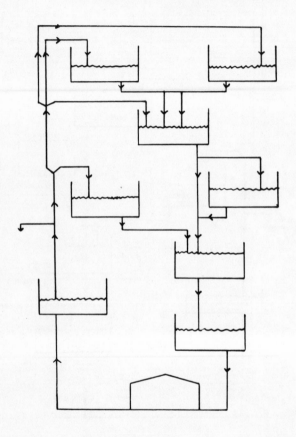

Debtors	Bank: Overdraft facility	Stock wastage
Trade creditors	Actual account	Pump house
Fixed assets	Bad debts	Owner and lenders
Stocks	Wages and other cash expenses	Gross profit margin
	Money in from debtors	

when pumped via the financial control pump house which is powered by budgets, cash flow forecasts, stock control, etc.

Money in from debtors

This is a temporary holding tank only included to emphasise how sales are only cash once debts are collected. From this tank payments are made for cash expenses and the other tanks are re-filled.

Trade credit tank

If suppliers get their money regularly, this will continue its gravity feed which finances stocks. But should an interruption in supply from 'Money in from debtors' occur, it will quickly run dry as creditors withdraw facilities.

Bank account

Finally, the Bank account tank is replenished. This has three sources of supply:

(1) retained profit
(2) owner's capital (in shares or loans)
(3) bank overdraft or other loans.

Both the owner's and the bank's tanks need periodic replenishment if they are to be able and willing to continue providing the extra finance which is needed as inflation raises stock values, etc, let alone to pay for expansion.

Too much cash in one tank reduces the cash available elsewhere

Since the cash supply in the business is limited an excess in one tank must drain off from another, perhaps causing a shortage. The excess may be caused by poor control of spending decisions or by failure to collect debts. This reflects itself in the various ratios previously discussed.

What are the financial decisions made in your organisation? Who takes them?

These are catch questions to see whether the previous message has sunk in! Before continuing, consider how the money is spent in your business and who takes the decisions. Refer back to the water tank chart when working out your answers and write them down here under the headings:

Decisions   Who takes them?

The decisions are made thus

The decision is irrevocable once the order is placed for an asset, such as a piece of equipment, a vehicle, etc, or for goods or materials for re-sale or use in manufacture. Once a sale is made on credit to a customer, cash has been committed to that deal.

These are the points at which the commitment is made. The subsequent payment is inevitable sooner or later. Cash management must therefore start with control over the placing of orders. The management of the accounts payable (creditors) ledger, or invoices outstanding, can be helpful, particularly in squeezing a little extra credit when money is particularly tight, but it is really only tinkering with the problem. Once the order is placed it is usually too late to avert the need to make the payment.

The third expenditure point listed, that of granting credit to customers, is not the same as the others. No actual payment is made; on the contrary, money is subsequently received from the customer. Nevertheless, there is a very real cost involved in granting credit. This is not just a question of the interest charges on the money which is outstanding. Every time goods go out of the business on credit, they have to be replaced by other goods in order to maintain stocks. Frequently it is not the production manager or the buyer who initiates an order for goods or materials in the first place, but the sales manager who creates the need to buy in further supplies by making the credit sale in the first place.

Whether these jobs are all done by one man or by a team of people, it is important to understand how the different decisions interlock with each other.

Naturally, one would not want to overstress the spending of money by the sales manager when he grants credit. His job, after all, is to obtain sales. However, he should understand that the responsibility for operating the company's credit policy starts primarily with him and that this is not just a red tape procedure set up for the benefit of the accounts department.

The arithmetic of credit control

This may be a good point at which to demonstrate the arithmetic involved in a bad debt. If your gross profit is 30 per cent you have materials and direct expenses in a £100 bad debt value £70. To recover that loss of £70, you will therefore need to make a further £230 of sales. This is bad enough, but consider the situation if you take the net profit on sale. Since the collection of the money from the customer is the last operation in the whole chain of events, it is reasonable to charge on to a sale more than just the direct cost of producing the goods or the services. After paying all the overheads, salaries, etc of the business, many net profits are no more than 10 per cent or less of the sales value. To recover the real loss on a bad debt of £100 at a net profit margin of 10 per cent, ie £90, you will need to make no less than £900 of new sales.

Even if you argue that this overstates the case because the administrative and other overhead costs will not increase in proportion to the extra sales required to recover the bad debt, the true increase in sales needed to cover the bad debt must surely lie at least halfway between the two figures, ie between £500 and £600.

The executive team

I hope that I have now persuaded you that the financial decisions in your business are not taken by just one person. It is the entire executive team which is involved.

Even in the very smallest organisation this is true. The small shopkeeper does not have executives as such, but his staff are, or should be, involved in taking stock and keeping track of goods required, etc. However small you are, if you have not managed to involve your staff to the extent that they understand the importance of minimising stocks, having the right goods to hand to meet customers' requirements, etc and take an active part in helping you to achieve those objectives, you are not running your business at its maximum effectiveness.

In the larger organisation, the team may consist of one or more of the following executive staff:

Buyer
Production manager
Development manager
Research manager
Despatch manager
Head storeman
Sales manager
and, of course, The Boss.

Why the research manager?

This applies only to those readers whose businesses spend a significant sum of money each year on research and development (R and D) of one kind or another. These businesses should have a sub-heading or division of the fixed assets tank in the water tank chart between fixed assets and research and development.

Research and development is a tank of enormous size into which huge sums can flow with no resulting value whatever.

The problem of R and D is always to make it start

producing cash. This is not a matter of 'as quickly as possible', so much as 'within reasonable time'. The scientist or technician always wants to perfect his product before putting it on the market. This is in direct conflict with the need of the organisation, which is to get some cash coming in to offset the continuing expenditure.

R and D produces a product, which generates cash to pay for the continuing cost of improving. It is very valuable to the company. R and D which simply absorbs cash over an indefinite period in indefinite amounts may very well destroy the company. However good the potential, however technically exciting the project, future possibilities never paid current bills.

Are your priorities muddled?

Cash is 'spent' by the people who order things or who grant credit to customers, not when cheques are signed. Often orders, particularly for stock items, are initiated by junior staff who are ignorant of policy decisions on product development, discontinuing of lines, etc. Resulting mistakes can tie up money in surplus or unusable stocks.

Yet the purchase of a typewriter often requires the approval of the managing director. The potential loss is very small; his secretary understands typewriters better and, even if she got it wrong, the machine could be sold quickly at a limited loss. How many muddled priorities like this are there in your organisation?

Section 12:
Simple Business Calculations

This section explains some basic business calculations, with which many people have difficulty.

Percentages

To find what percentage 40 is of 320 divide thus:

$$\frac{40}{320} = 0.125$$

Move the decimal point two places right and you have the percentage, ie 12½%. Prove this to yourself thus:

10 on 100 is 10%: $\frac{10}{100} = .10 = 10\%$.

Profit mark-up

Mark-up is the percentage profit based on cost.

Profit margin

Margin is the percentage profit based on selling price.

Comparison of mark-up and margin

The same sum of profit is a lower percentage when expressed as a profit margin than it is when calculated as a profit mark-up. Some examples are given in the table below.

Many people confuse both themselves and others by not being clear as to whether they are quoting a mark-up or a margin. 100 per cent has to be a mark-up, because one cannot have a sale price which is all profit. 25 per cent could easily be either, and you should make sure which is meant.

Cost £	Profit £	Selling price £	Mark-up	Fraction	Margin	Fraction
100	100	200	100%	1	50%	$\frac{1}{2}$
100	50	150	50%	$\frac{1}{2}$	33.3%	$\frac{1}{3}$
100	25	125	25%	$\frac{1}{4}$	20%	$\frac{1}{5}$
100	80	180	80%	$\frac{4}{5}$	44.4%	$\frac{4}{9}$

Note that a mark-up fraction can be converted to a margin fraction by adding the numerator (top half) to the denominator (bottom half). The top half stays the same. Thus a mark-up of $\frac{1}{2}$ is a margin of $\frac{1}{3}$, $\frac{4}{5}$ becomes $\frac{4}{9}$ and so on.

Which to use — mark-up or margin?

When pricing individual articles, you use mark-up because you know the cost and you are calculating the selling price.

When discussing the average gross profit you obtain overall, however, it is better to think in margin terms. You know your total sales — what is in the till or on your invoices. You do not usually know your total cost of goods sold without drawing up accounts. So in calculating total profits it is easier to work out margin on sales than mark-up on cost.

In pricing individual products, use cost and calculate mark-ups. Once you have decided your policy on either mark-up or margin, the other ratio follows. Naturally an average mark-up of 50% will not produce an actual margin of $33\frac{1}{3}$% because of stock losses of various kinds.

For example, a retail boutique may mark-up at 100%: ie a margin of 50%. But it will probably not achieve an actual margin much above 35 — 40%, depending upon how skilfully the owner buys. There is always unsold stock to be cleared at reduced prices, plus pilferage, etc, which cuts the actual margin obtained.

Eliminate VAT

If VAT applies, it must be taken out of both cost and sales prices to get the true profit margin. If all your sales are at the same VAT rate, it does not matter if you calculate your margin on a sales price including VAT, providing you do the same for all goods. If you sell at more than one rate, your margins will not be comparable unless you eliminate VAT.

To calculate the selling price net of VAT

If the net price subject to VAT at 8% is 100, that including VAT is 108.

Thus, if the price including VAT is £2.50: $\frac{100}{108}$ x £2.50 = £2.315 which is the net price.

Proof: £2.50 − £2.31½ is 18½p which is the VAT at 8% on £2.31½.

To calculate a selling price for an item at a given percentage margin

If you buy at 50 and you wish to earn a 30% margin on your selling price net of VAT, the calculation of your selling price is thus:

Selling price net of VAT is 100: 30% profit gives a cost of 70 so multiply your cost by $\frac{100}{70}$

Thus: $\frac{100}{70}$ x 50 = 71.43p. Proof: profit is 21.43 and $\frac{21.43}{71.43}$ = 30%.

Add VAT at 8% on 71.43 = 5.71.

Total 77.14 so you round down to 77p or up to 77½p or 78p to give your selling price including VAT.

Alternatively, your margin of 30% = $\frac{3}{10}$. This is a mark-up of $\frac{3}{7}$.

$\frac{3}{7}$ x 50 = 21.43, the same cash profit as above.

Questions involving simple business calculations

(Answers below)

Here are some questions to test your understanding of the various ratios previously discussed.

(a) What must your sales be for you to break even if your fixed costs and your gross profits are as below?

Fixed costs	*Gross profit*
(i) £100 per week	20% margin
(ii) £100 per week	20% mark-up
(iii) £330 per week	30% margin
(iv) £330 per week	30% mark-up
(v) £330 per week	$\frac{2}{3}$ margin
(vi) £330 per week	$\frac{2}{3}$ mark-up

(b) Your sales are £40000 per annum and your gross profit 25 per cent. If you cut your prices by 5 per cent how much sales must you add in order to make the same profit?

(c) If you raise your prices by 5 per cent how much sales could you afford to lose before you reduce your profits?

(d) Your stocks are £5000 at cost and you turn them over 7 times. What is your cost of sales?
Your margin is 20 per cent. What is the value of your sales?

Answers to questions involving simple business calculations

(a) (i) $100 \times \frac{100}{20} = £500$ per week

(ii) $\frac{1}{5}$ mark-up $= \frac{1}{6}$ margin (16.67%)

100×6 (or $100 \times \frac{100}{16.67}$) $= £600$ per week

(iii) $330 \times \frac{100}{30} = £1100$ per week

(iv) $\frac{3}{10}$ mark-up = $\frac{3}{13}$ margin

$330 \times \frac{13}{3} = £1430$ per week

(v) $330 \times \frac{3}{2} = £495$

(vi) $\frac{2}{3}$ mark-up = $\frac{2}{5}$ margin

$330 \times \frac{5}{2} = £825$ per week

(b) Your price cut will cost 5% on £40000 = £2000. You must earn this by extra sales at the new gross profit, ie

$£2000 \times \frac{100}{20} = £10000$ extra sales needed, an increase of 25%.

(c) Your price increase will earn 5% on £40000 = £2000. You can lose sales at the new gross profit thus:

$£2000 \times \frac{100}{30} = £6667$, a decrease of 16.7%.

Alternative calculations are to apply the new gross profit margins to the gross profit sum required which gives the new sales figures.

Thus (b) $£10000 \times \frac{100}{20} = £50000$

(c) $£10000 \times \frac{100}{30} = £33333$

(d) Stocks of £5000 turned over 7 times = cost of sales £35000. If the margin is 20% ($\frac{1}{5}$) mark-up is ¼. ¼ x £35000 = £8750 profit.

Sales are therefore £43750.

Section 13:
The Key Facts about Your Business Finances

The facts shown by your accounts

Previous sections have mentioned a variety of ratios. These are summarised at the end of this section and some questions and exercises given to help you fix them in your mind.

It has been said that the key points about choosing a retail shop are site, site and site. Of running a business one could say they are gross profit, gross profit and cash, cash, cash.

Gross profit is of such significance in relation to net profit that it usually dwarfs all other profit and loss figures. Refer back to Section 9 to revise this point.

Cash is so vital because it pays the bills. The previous section showing the cash flow chart emphasises this.

Taken together, the various ratios tell you all you need to know about the financial side of your business.

What are the key facts not shown by your accounts?

So far we have discussed the ratios which are shown by either the profit and loss account or the balance sheet. However, not all important information is shown by these two documents.

What is a key operating ratio?

Key operating ratios measure facts which matter about your daily trading, ie the activities which have a significant effect upon net profit. Examples are percentage labour efficiency and sales per square foot. Others are listed below.

Operating ratios therefore measure details on a daily or weekly basis in contrast to profit and loss or balance sheet ratios which measure overall results annually. They are vital because if daily operations are not right, the annual profit will not be either.

Which are your particular key operating ratios?

This depends upon your trade. Most operating ratios concern either sales, manufacturing output, gross profit or labour use since these are usually the key figures affecting profit. In retailing, for example, gross profit earned per product and per square foot of space and unit sales per product are key facts, whilst in a motor repair workshop it is the labour hours charged weekly to customers as a percentage of those paid to staff.

Some examples of key operating ratios

- Stock wastage in all its forms
- Labour hours sold as a percentage of labour hours paid for
- Overtime
- Sales per square foot
- Manufacturing efficiency ie output rates per hour or per pound of wages etc, output per unit of fuel consumption or pound of capital investment, etc
- Warehouse efficiency, ie tonnages shifted, etc
- Vehicle running costs per mile or per ton mile or per salesman
- Salesman's costs per salesman or per sales call

This list cannot be comprehensive since the range of businesses is so huge. What matters depends upon your particular circumstances. With a little thought, combined with an understanding of how the main figures in your profit and loss account and balance sheet relate to each other, you should have no difficulty in identifying the ratios which matter to you.

Where do the ratios come from?

Many of the above ratios not shown on the balance sheet or profit and loss account will be available from management reports. It is important that the reporting system, which produces the figures for comparison of actual results against budget includes such key ratios. It is often more meaningful to everybody concerned to talk in unit volumes per day or per hour than in money values.

When does VAT affect ratios?

VAT is extracted from all figures in the profit and loss account because it is neither a cost nor an income, the net difference being paid to the Government.

But VAT does appear in the balance sheet. It is part of what your debtors owe you and what you owe your creditors and is therefore included in the figures for these items. Section 10 illustrates the need to adjust for VAT when calculating the respective ratios for debtors and creditors.

The Government may itself be a creditor or a debtor for VAT. If it is included in debtors or creditors, any such balance owing to or from the Government must be extracted before calculating the ratios.

The stock valuation does not include VAT because the VAT paid has already been recovered. Its ratio is therefore not affected.

If you are using sales or purchase figures from your records rather than from your annual accounts, make sure whether or not VAT should be included and adjust as necessary.

How do I judge whether my ratios are good or bad?

There are no hard and fast rules. Businesses vary so much, even within the same trade, that what is a good figure for one may be only average for another. For example, of two concerns, one may sell largely to local authorities or other Government organisations who are safe but slow payers. That company inevitably will have to give longer credit than the other. This is one of the problems of doing business with those customers, which is perhaps balanced by the advantage of steady secure orders.

Comparisons with other businesses in the same trade are usually helpful. Often the average for a given ratio, such as gross profit or stocks, is fairly well established. Before reaching conclusions based on such comparisons, consider whether all the factors involved are similar. For example, a high gross profit margin usually means efficiency, but it can also reflect high prices and poor value to the customer. In a restaurant, one can improve margins by cutting the size of the portions or the quality of the raw materials but such policies can quickly alienate the customers.

The stocks ratio can also vary considerably as a result of policy. A heavy stockholding can reflect a business built upon service; the rapid supply of technical spare parts is an example. Provided the profit margins are high enough, such a policy can be profitable.

For example, a stock of £1000 at cost turned over three times (ie an average holding of four months) means a cost of sales of £3000. At a gross margin of 50 per cent this means sales of £6000 and gross profit of £3000. If the stock turns over six times, but at a gross margin of only 25 per cent, the cost of sales will be £6000, sales £8000 and gross profit £2000. To make the same gross profit of £3000 at 25 per cent margin, sales must be £12000 which means a cost of sales of £9000 and a stock turn of nine.

A gross margin of 50 per cent is of course much higher than that in many trades but the example illustrates how the arithmetic works. It is possible to make profits from stocking slow-moving goods in a wide range if the margins are big enough. Manufacturers may well make gross margins as high as 50 per cent but they will usually have heavy promotional and selling expenses which drastically cut into their margins and which make it essential to work on lower stock levels.

Interfirm comparison schemes

Many trade associations run interfirm comparison schemes and there is also the Centre for Interfirm Comparisons.

Such schemes provide valuable information on a range of key ratios and can show you how your business compares. In highlighting those of your figures which are above or below the average for your industry, they can help you identify and concentrate on those aspects of your business which most need attention.

Your own ratios over a period

One of the most useful comparisons can be your own ratios over a three-year period, for example, provided that the basis of the figures has remained similar and that your business has not radically altered in its nature. Such comparisons can show up trends which are free from the inevitable distortions caused by the differing nature of other businesses.

Use your commonsense!

Some ratios relate directly to your own policies and business. For instance, is your debtors sales ratio in line with your policy on credit to customers? But think first. Do you have cash sales or a large chunk of business on different terms which mean that the figures need adjusting before calculating the ratio?

Are you using trade credit correctly?

If you are not taking full normal credit, you are settling your bills before you need to. Perhaps settlement discount made this worthwhile. If you obtain 2½ per cent on £100 each month if you pay in seven days, your annual cash discount adds up to £30. If normal settlement terms are one month, you are paying £100 three weeks early. This is an average of £75 tied up throughout the year on which your £30 is 40 per cent — well worthwhile!

If, on the other hand, you are taking more trade credit than you should, you risk straining the goodwill of your suppliers. Push them too far and they may stop all credit. Extended credit should be used in emergencies only, not as a regular practice; you are in bad trouble if something does alarm your creditors and they clamp down.

Are you earning enough to stay in business?

Your ratios may be better than the average for your industry but are they good enough? It is no good being the best in your sector if this merely means that, in a declining industry, you are losing ground more slowly than the rest.

In the long term, to stay in business, you must earn enough on the money tied up not only to pay the interest but also to finance the replacement of assets and the development of the business. If money comes from the bank, you must pay interest. If you or your shareholders, provide it, you and they need an adequate return. Over and above this, however, you must invest in new equipment, etc at inflated prices and you must finance growth in sales, development into new products, etc. If you do not, your business will decline. It may be slow; it may take many years, but it will happen. Low profitability means low investment, minimal maintenance of existing installations and so on.

Then one day you have to re-equip or to launch a major new investment in order to compete at all. By this time overall profitability is so low that it cannot cover the interest costs of borrowing to finance the new project at inflated prices. So do not kid yourself that you can always borrow new capital. In the end, the key to survival is adequate rates of return of profit on net capital employed. Remember that, as explained in Section 8, my definition of this includes the bank overdraft and any long-term loans, interest being added back to the profit, since this is all the money permanently or semi-permanently in use.

Exercises on profit and loss and balance sheet ratios

Exercise 1 *(Answers overleaf)*

You have learnt various ratios in previous sections. Each, when applied to one figure will produce another as illustrated in the question in Section 12. Use the information given below to fill in the blank spaces. Ignore VAT.

	A	B	C	D
Sales	£8000			
Gross profit	£2000			£4000
Stock ratio	6	8	4	
Mark-up %			80%	
Margin %				20%
Stocks at cost		£5000	£2000	£4000
Stocks at selling		£7500		
Debtors ratio	8	6		
Debtors value			£1000	£2000
Creditors ratio	3	4		5
Creditors value			£500	

To simplify the arithmetic for you, the stocks, debtors and creditors are expressed here as ratios rather than weeks or months of throughput. Thus a stock ratio of 6 represents $\frac{52}{6}$ = 8.²/3 weeks sales. It is often more meaningful to think in weeks which is why this method has been used in the previous sections in preference to numerical ratios. For the purposes of this question, assume creditors relate to cost of sales.

Exercise 2 *(Answers overleaf)*

In Exercise 1 the creditors ratio was applied to cost of sales in order not to make the question too cumbersome. However, it really relates to goods purchased. Purchases vary from cost of sales according to whether stocks have increased or decreased. This exercise illustrates the point. Fill in the missing figures.

	A	B	C	D
	£	£	£	£
Opening stocks	4000		18000	11000
Purchases	20000	14000		63000
Closing stocks	5000	7000	26000	
Cost of sales		17000	104000	45000

Answers to Exercise 1

	A	B	C	D
Sales	£8000	£60000	£14400	£20000
Gross profit	£2000	£20000	£6400	£4000
Stock ratio	6	8	4	4
Mark-up %	33⅓ %	50%	80%	25%
Margin %	25%	33⅓ %	44.4%	20%
Stocks at cost	£1000	£5000	£2000	£4000
Stocks at selling	£1333	£7500	£3600	£5000
Debtors ratio	8	6	14.4	10
Debtors value	£1000	£10000	£1000	£2000
Creditors ratio	3	4	16	5
Creditors value	£2000	£10000	£500	£3200

Column A

Gross profit to sales = margin 25% or ¼

Therefore mark-up $\frac{1}{3}$

Cost of goods £8000 − £2000 = £6000. Stockturn 6 so stocks at cost £1000

Sales £8000: stockturn 6: stocks at selling = $\frac{8000}{6}$ = £1333.

Debtors = $\dfrac{\text{sales } 8000}{\text{ratio } 8}$ = £1000

Creditors = $\dfrac{\text{cost of goods £6000}}{\text{ratio } 3}$ = £2000

Column B

Stocks at selling £7500 x stockturn 8 = sales £60000
Stocks at cost £5000 so profit in stocks £2500. Therefore mark-up 50%; margin $33\frac{1}{3}$ %

Margin $33\frac{1}{3}$ % on sales = £20000

$\dfrac{\text{Sales}}{\text{Debtors ratio}}$ = debtors £10000

$\dfrac{\text{Cost of sales}}{\text{Creditors ratio}}$ (£60000 − £20000 = £40000) = creditors £10000

Column C

Mark-up $\dfrac{4}{5}$ so margin $\dfrac{4}{9}$ = 44.4%

Stocks at cost £2000 + mark-up 80% = stocks at selling £3600

Stocks at selling x stock ratio 4 = sales £14400

Cost of sales = stocks at cost x stock ratio = £8000

Gross profit either mark-up x cost of sales or margin x sales = £6400

Debtors ratio = $\dfrac{\text{sales}}{\text{debtors value}}$ = £1000

Creditors ratio = $\dfrac{\text{cost of sales}}{\text{creditors value}}$ = 16

Column D

Gross profit £4000 at margin $\dfrac{1}{5}$ = sales £20000

Margin $\dfrac{1}{5}$ so mark-up $\dfrac{1}{4}$ or 25%

Stocks at cost £4000 + mark-up 25% = stocks at selling £5000

$\dfrac{\text{Sales}}{\text{Stocks at selling}}$ = stock ratio 4 (or $\dfrac{\text{cost of sales}}{\text{stocks at cost}}$)

$\dfrac{\text{Sales}}{\text{Debtors}}$ = debtors ratio 10

Sales − gross profit = cost of sales: $\dfrac{\text{cost of sales}}{\text{creditors ratio}}$ = creditors £3200

Answers to Exercise 2

A   4000 + 20000 − 5000 = £19000 cost of sales

B   17000 + 7000 − 14000 = £10000 opening stocks

C   104000 + 26000 − 18000 = £112000 purchases

D   11000 + 63000 − 45000 = £29000 closing stocks

Summary of the vital facts about your business

Key ratios shown by the profit and loss account	*Expressed in*
Gross profit	%
Wages and salaries to sales	%
Principal expenses to sales	%
Net profit to sales	%

Key ratios shown by the balance sheet	
Current assets to current liabilities	Ratio
Liquidity − the acid test	Ratio

Key ratios shown by the profit and loss account and balance sheet combined	
Debtors to sales	Days
Stocks to usage	Days
Creditors to purchases and expenses	Days
Net profit to net capital employed	%
Super profit to proprietor's interest	%

Key operating ratios
   See page 88 for some examples

Questions on Section 13

☐ *Why does each of these ratios matter?*

☐ *What are the profit and loss and balance sheet ratios of your own business?*
   Pause here and look at your own accounts. Fill in your own ratios in the spaces provided above. This will teach you invaluable facts about your business.

☐ *What are the key operating ratios for your particular business?*
   Write them below with actual figures if possible.
